The Fool's Journey through the Tarot

~ Pentacles ~

2nd Edition

by Noel Eastwood

Book 2 The Fool's Journey Series

All rights reserved, copyright © 2018 and 2020 2nd Edition Noel Eastwood

Noel Eastwood asserts the moral right to be identified as the author of this work. By payment of the required fees, you have been granted the non-exclusive and non-transferable right to access and read the text of this ebook on screen or in print form. No part of the text may be reproduced, transmitted, downloaded, decompiled, reverse engineered, stored in or introduced into any information storage or retrieval system, in any form or by any means, electronic or mechanical, known or otherwise yet invented, without the express permission of Noel Eastwood.

This novel is a work of fiction set in the context of Tarot and other esoteric wisdom. Characterisation, incidents and locations portrayed are the work of the author's imagination. No affiliation is implied or intended with any organisation or recognisable body mentioned within.

> To contact the author, Noel Eastwood:
> Email: info@plutoscave.com
> Web: http://www.plutoscave.com
> Facebook: @PlutosCave
> Editor: Kristal
> Editor: 2nd Edition: JoAnn
> Cover: JoAnn
> Deck: Original Rider-Waite deck (1910)

I dedicate this work to my beloved wife, Marja, for whose patience, understanding and proofreading I am most grateful. Thank you to Krystal and the beta readers of the first edition. Finally, thank you to JoAnn for her cover design and her endless hours of editing the 2nd Edition with the new material.

View the map online at **www.plutoscave.com**

INTRODUCTION

In this book Follin continues his journey through the Tarot, living and working in the Pentacles Kingdom. This 2nd Edition has been carefully edited and I have included new material that further illustrates the Pentacles suit.

The Suit of Pentacles is essentially about the physical world. While it includes material possessions and wealth it also refers to family, work, health, giving and receiving. It addresses building, growing, creating and pragmatism. It relates to achievement through goal setting and mindfulness and the temptations of overindulgence. It includes the relation of input, i.e. attention, time, money and labour, to outcomes. The elemental theme of Pentacles is Earth.

Once again, this is not a recipe book of Tarot interpretations, but a story in which the Tarot archetypes and meanings are interwoven.

The characters and their stories illustrate various cards and their meanings. The meditations demonstrate how to access each Tarot symbol and archetype.

I have drawn from the wisdom and techniques of many esoteric practices to which I been exposed over the past forty-five years. Initially I hesitated to use anything from sources I could not clearly acknowledge. Then I realized that knowledge and understanding are meant to be shared. I have included what I believe to be of value to the reader.

There is no single correct way to interpret the cards, just as there is no single interpretation of the symbolism and imagery evoked by the Tarot. Your interpretation may be quite different from mine, and that is fine.

I hope that you enjoy this next stage of Follin's life and that it helps you along your own path, whether that be in Tarot interpretation or the wider arena of personal development.

Noel Eastwood, Canberra, Australia
September 2020

Prologue

Eve returned home just as the sun was setting. On the back porch she strung up the herbs she had gathered that day. She took off her cloak and heavy boots.

"Follin, I'm home," she called out as she did each evening to an empty silence. As she went inside she noticed that the cottage was warm and that the banked fire in the grate still glowed.

'Must be this new wood,' she thought.

She stoked the fire and swung the kettle over it. The candle on the table needed replacing so she went to the cupboard in the hall. As she lit her candle, Eve heard a soft sound coming from her bedroom.

'Next door's cat asleep on my bed again,' she thought.

"Come on, time to go home," Eve said as she entered the bedroom to shoo him off.

"But I am home," said a sleepy voice from the bed.

—

ACE OF PENTACLES

Embarking on an earthly adventure.

Eve had wiped away her tears as she lay the flower wreath on her little sister's grave. It was this final act that cemented her conviction to leave behind the remains of her past and set out on her own journey. It felt like the end of life but, in reality, it was the beginning, sparked by her first meeting with Follin, some years earlier. They had met at the crossroads on the outskirts of her village. He had looked so lost and confused that Eve had no choice but to feel sorry for this handsome, yet fragile, young man. The memory of sitting in the grass together, eating her lunch and talking of life and the future, had remained with her.

At that time there was a wary peace in the Mystic Isles. She lived with her parents in the village and when her parents were away from home, Eve and her little sister, Gabriela, would stay with their grandparents in the forest. Things were simple then, life held few complications and she was happy.

She and Follin were both just kids, barely out of puberty, when they had first met. The spark that ignited at the moment of their meeting had continued to burn.

Eve often returned to the place where they had met: a grassy glade beside the forest track near her grandparents' house.

"Oh, Follin, where are you now? I need you so much," she would sigh, sitting alone in the grass, twirling a golden dandelion flower, staring into space.

It was there, sitting in the grass, that she had recalled Follin saying he lived on the edge of the deep forest in the south of the Mystic Isle. It was a small village, right on the edge of the island. She was an Isle girl herself. Her home was in the far north-east, where the Wildlanders often landed to make raids on the villages. Eve had joked that they both were half Wildlander and half Mystic Islander, harbouring wild magic of all the elements.

Follin had told her that he was on a journey to find his father, or, perhaps, it was to find himself. Eve saw that he did not know where he was heading. He had mentioned some of the people he had met on his journey and told her of some of his adventures. She had sat entranced as he spoke - his was a true adventure of the spirit that she now yearned for.

Eve recalled him telling her about his brother who had died from the plague, brought by invaders some years earlier. This crippled his father who had fought to prevent the sickness ravaging his beloved isle, but he could not prevent it ravaging his own family. The shy young man had then described how his family struggled to survive after his father abandoned them - a broken man.

Follin had told her that his father was a mage, well known in the Mystic Isles and in the outer kingdoms – even the Wildlands. But he was powerless to save his own son. No longer able to live with himself, his father disappeared, to where no one knew. In some ways Follin's own journey was to understand his father, to find his father's legacy within himself.

The Lovers had met just the once, some years ago. Where Follin went next, she had no idea. All she could think of was to find him, not that it made any sense, she thought. She remembered the name of his village, '*Saoirse*'. Follin had explained that it meant '*be true to yourself*', and that was what he was seeking on his journey – his true self.

Soon after her meeting with Follin the north was invaded. Eve's father and mother were taken to serve in the army and died shortly afterward. She had tried to make ends meet for herself and her little sister but the war made it almost impossible to survive. After the invaders had pillaged and plundered the countryside the islanders began to starve.

Her once friendly neighbours became competitors for food and resources - if they could gain an advantage over another to feed their families, they would. To Eve's horror, she saw loyal islanders betray their friends for security and food from the enemy soldiers. She witnessed neighbours who had once invited their friends to break bread at their table now readily betray them to survive. The world she thought she knew was gone, replaced by a violent, bitter world where friends became enemies.

Eve had tried to help where she could. She had learned enough healing from her grandparents and parents to be of use to the community. It was one way she could earn enough to feed herself and her little sister. But her knowledge and skill in healing was not enough when disease soon followed starvation. The invasion had laid waste to everything she knew and loved.

In that final act of laying flowers on Gabriela's grave, Eve realised that finding Follin was her last reason to stay alive.

"So that's when you came looking for me?" asked Follin, his eyes red from his tears as she related her story.

"Yes. I remembered the name of your village and the directions you gave me. That's how I found my way here." It was still too early to get out of bed so they lay together, cherishing the warmth of their bodies against each other.

"I'm so sorry, Eve. If I had known what you were destined to experience I would have come looking for you earlier." He pulled her closer then kissed her wet cheeks.

Follin had just arrived from his sojourn in the Tarot Empire with the Major Arcana, this was only their second morning together. There was so much to catch up on since their first meeting almost four years ago.

"You don't know where your mother and sister went either, do you, Follin?" Eve leaned on one elbow to look at him. She recognised that her lover had also lost so much while he was away.

"No, I don't know where they are. My father left when I was about ten, since then all I've known is hardship. I blamed myself for his leaving, but I now know that he had his own demons to conquer." Follin sniffed back tears threatening to flood his eyes. "I've seen his childhood, and the horrors he lived through, in my meditations. The fighting, witnessing his own family taken... what is it about humans that we do such terrible things to each other?"

Eve pulled her hand from the warm covers and placed it on his cheek. She followed the path of tears from his eyes to his throat then kissed him again.

"My love, it seems we are destined to repeat the same horrors year after year, lifetime after lifetime. The day they took my parents to serve in the war I was staying with my grandparents in the mountains. When I arrived home, Gabriela came out of hiding and told me what had happened. They were such good people, they didn't deserve to be taken away from us." Eve stopped to look up at the thatched ceiling. She watched several mice run along the beams above. They had been her daily companions since she had arrived there. Seeing them always gave her comfort.

"We lost nearly all the food in our larder, and the chickens, they were all taken by our own soldiers. Then the enemy soldiers came and took the last of what we'd hidden. It was at night, we could see the fires in the distance. They burnt my village. I took Gabriela to hide in the forest where we lived on herbs, mushrooms and roots. When the soldiers had gone we came back to find almost everyone dead and our house burned to the ground. Later I heard a rumour that my grandparents had fled but no one knew where."

"How did you survive?" Follin could feel her heart beating against his chest.

Eve smiled when she remembered her little sister, how brave Gabriela was, but then her face clouded over as she continued the story. "The soldiers left their dead behind and the smell of all those bodies was horrible. We went through their clothing looking for food. We found some stale bread, barely enough to last for a few days. Then Gabriela became sick. The soldiers had brought the plague with them and left it behind for us. Our neighbours who had hidden in the forest with us died, too. I was the only one who didn't get sick. I don't know why I was saved, but I was left alive when I should have died. I wanted to die. I was so scared and so alone." She turned and stared into Follin's bright eyes. "You know what saved me?" she asked.

Follin shook his head.

"You," she said.

"What? Me? But I wasn't there," he said, surprised.

"All I could think of was being with you. That's what kept me going, that's what kept me alive. I searched and searched until I found your village. I asked the gatekeeper where you lived and he warned me that your family had long gone and the house was falling apart. I wasn't afraid, I knew you would find me." Eve dropped her head back onto the pillow.

"I had dreams of being with you, Eve. I saw you asleep on this bed, in my arms, just like now. I saw it so many times it felt real," he told her.

Follin felt Eve withdraw from him.

"Follin," Eve said in a quiet voice. "There's something else I need to tell you."

'Yes?" he said and waited. Eve was silent. Follin drew her back to him and kissed her forehead. "What is it, my love?"

"You need to know that I told the gatekeeper that I am your wife. I thought the villagers wouldn't let me live here otherwise. I told them that we were married in my village up north, that then we were separated and you had told me to come here and wait for you."

"Wife, huh?" laughed Follin. He had seen Eve as his wife many times in his dreams. "Do you really want to be my wife?" he asked.

"Yes," replied Eve, "ever since we met."

Follin stretched and said, "Well, then, we'd better go see the Mayor and ask him to put our marriage into the Saoirse records. Then we'll visit the head families of the town. I'm sure to find some sort of work with them. They should be happy with the healing you've done with their families. You'll be a good luck charm for me. When I left home all those years ago I was a fool, but now I think I've grown up a bit." He smiled. "And I'm married now, too."

———

Follin had been absent from the village on his mystics quest for seven years. Despite the devastation of the wars, and the plague that followed, there were still enough people in the township who remembered the awkward, gangly fool who could not read, write nor catch a ball. Today Follin walked tall, his head held high as he walked with his wife through the middle of town. At the third house his inquiries for work met with success.

"Well, well, well, it is young Follin. I see you've returned to your family home and married that lovely young healer girl. She has become a valued member of our township. Not only have you grown and filled out but you seem to have matured somewhat. I have heard that you now know a little of your numbers and letters, and that you have a way with people, too." The aged Knight, Sir Cecil, smiled lightly. "I may have some work for you. My House Steward has taken ill and I need someone to manage my household. Be here tomorrow at dawn and you can start with managing the day staff for me. They can be a bit of a handful and they'll play tricks, but if you're the man for the job, you'll have them to their tasks soon enough. If not, then I'll know about it by lunchtime." Sir Cecil looked at the young man steadily.

Follin held his gaze. "Thank you, sir," he said firmly and walked briskly out of the building to join Eve waiting at the tavern.

"And so? Did Sir Cecil give you a job?" Eve's head was tilted to one side and a questioning smile played across her face. When Follin failed to answer straight away her smile was quickly followed by a worried frown.

It was Follin's turn to smile. "Of course he did. Have you no faith, my dearest? I'm to try out as House Steward and manage Sir Cecil's household staff," he replied with a grin. Together they chatted over their hot coffee, a new beverage, brought in by seagoing traders. It was strangely invigorating but horrid in taste. Putting his cup down Follin politely said, "Dearest, next time, can we just have tea?"

The days were long as Follin worked hard to solve the many and varied problems of Sir Cecil's household. At first the staff were not happy with their new washerwoman; next, it was the squabbles amongst the younger staff and the older staff, followed by a stream of complaints of one form or another. Each was met by Follin with a logical application of firm but empathic instruction. By the end of his second week, Sir Cecil called Follin in for what he thought would be a review of his performance.

"Son," he said, "you've performed extremely well. I deliberately threw you into the deep end and you've come up trumps. Sadly, I have just received an urgent request for your services. I believe you will receive an important visitor very soon. It is with much regret that I have to let you go." Sir Cecil would not be pushed to give further explanation, only saying that a higher power, an old friend of his, had requested Follin's services.

The young man stood to shake the aged Knight's proffered hand, and sombrely made his way home. It was dark, it was cold, and he felt bewildered at this sudden turn of events. By the time he arrived home, Follin was frightened - no, he was terrified. What if this was just an excuse to get rid of him? What if Sir Cecil was really displeased with his performance but was too polite to tell him directly? What if this was all a terrible joke?

Follin walked into the cottage, changed into his work rags without speaking, then walked outside to weed the garden. He could not yet say a thing to Eve. He was afraid that what he feared most was true and then he would lose Eve, too. The sensitive young man needed time to think and he could do that best in the garden - alone.

A few minutes after Follin had left the house to contemplate his future, Eve heard a knock on the door. A dark-haired, well-presented young woman, a court Page, asked to speak with 'The Fool'.

"I'm sorry, but the only other person here is my husband, his name is Follin. How may I help you?" asked Eve, a little taken aback by the fine clothes and the formal manners of the pretty young lady at her front door.

"I have a message for... Follin, from an old friend of his, The Emperor," stated the Page.

Eve stood quietly as she considered the strange request. A few moments later she remembered her manners and invited her visitor inside. She took her to stand by the warm fire.

"I'll get my husband, he's outside tidying up the garden beds. Wait here, please, while I fetch him."

The young page studied the humble cottage and was pleased to see that it was well kept and clean. This was information that she would take back to her master. She was startled out of her reverie when she heard her name.

"Alice! Why, look at you, how you've grown. You were just a wee child the last time I saw you." Follin stepped forward to embrace the young lady warmly.

"Eve, this is Alice. She was one of the little girls running around the Empress' and Emperor's castle when I was there years ago." Follin spoke excitedly, this was such a surprise. "So what news do you bring? Is all well with my friends, the Empress and Emperor?"

Alice laughed as she was placed gently back on her feet. "Fool... I mean, Follin, it is lovely to see you again. All the girls still talk of that handsome young man who stole our hearts." She had begun to flirt with him but quickly remembered her assignment. "The Emperor instructed me to inform you that he wishes to see you as soon as possible. He also instructed me not to leave without you and your wife. We can leave as soon as you're both ready."

Eve looked at Page Alice, then at her husband. "We can't do that. I mean, we just got married, and now Follin has a very good job with Sir Cecil. If he doesn't turn up for work tomorrow he'll lose his one and only job. And besides," she paused to add with emphasis, "if he doesn't go to work tomorrow he'll never be trusted in the village again. We might as well kiss our home here goodbye."

Alice eyed Eve for a few seconds. "Eve, I was instructed to offer Follin employment with the Emperor himself. He said that he had positions for you both. He also asked me to tell you that you might not return to this village for some time if you accept his offer."

Both Follin and Eve stood, clearly perplexed, this didn't seem possible. A job offer from the Emperor?

Follin put his arm around his wife and pulled her in to his side protectively. "Alice, is this true? The Emperor wants to give us employment? We'll both be working for him in his castle? Did he say what we'll be doing?"

"Yes, he did say all that." The dark-haired Page gave a warm smile. "You'll be studying in each of the Tarot kingdoms, and Eve will be apprenticed to the alchemist, Mage Hermes, the Emperor's healer. Sir Cecil's letter commending your performance with his household has already arrived at the Emperor's castle. The Emperor was very pleased with his report. Follin, please, don't let this opportunity slip through your hands," she said, watching his reaction. She also watched Eve out of the corner of her eye.

Follin realised that he should have told Eve what Sir Cecil had said, but he had been afraid and confused. He breathed deeply and exhaled slowly. He repeated the act twice more as he settled the nervous butterflies fluttering in his stomach.

"Eve, my love, I was afraid to speak to you when I arrived home this evening," he began with a nervous rush of words. "Sir Cecil told me that he had to let me go from his employment because I was needed elsewhere. I was so worried that I didn't know what to do. That's why I went out to the gardens, to think and clear my mind."

Eve blinked then set her face ready for what might happen next. All this was so new to her that her own insecurities threatened to pierce her veil of calmness.

Follin turned to Alice. "Alice, would you care to share our evening meal?" He waited for her reply. When she nodded, he continued. "I need to meditate on this matter. The Empress often reminded me not to make an important decision in haste. I'll retire for just a short while to ponder before giving you my decision."

He turned to his wife once more. "I'm sorry if I upset you, dearest, I needed time alone. I would like to hear what you think before retiring to my meditation."

Eve was initially in mild shock, but now began to recover her senses on hearing her husband's explanation. "Husband of mine, whatever you decide to do I know it will prove to be the best thing for us. Personally, I can't wait."

Trying to suppress the growing excitement in her voice, Eve invited Alice to join her in preparing their evening meal. Follin smiled with relief as he walked outside to sit quietly in the woodshed to compose his mind.

'I'll contact the High Priestess and ask her for advice.'

As his breathing slowed he felt himself entering his personal sanctuary, a clearing in the forest. It was his old hermit cottage, a humble stone-walled hut with green grass sods covering its roof. He stopped to admire his handiwork: above the door was a carved oak beam showing a woman sitting beside a lion on a river bank.

He breathed slowly as he dropped deeper into trance. This time he found himself in the High Priestess's Sanctuary. He called softly for Hera, the High Priestess.

"It is The Fool who is not so foolish now. Welcome, Follin," he heard her soft, melodic voice inside his head, just as he had many times before. "I see you have come a long way. What do you wish from me?"

"High Priestess Hera, I've married a beautiful and honourable woman, I seek your blessing on our union," was his first request.

"You had it before you asked. What else do you request?"

"I have been invited to serve the Emperor, in his castle. Eve has been invited to study the art of healing with the Emperor's alchemist, Mage Hermes. I seek your wisdom on this."

"Ah, the Emperor. If it is his wish then it would be a wise act to join him in his household." The soft voice paused as she waited for Follin to process her words. "Now I have something to ask of you in return." Follin felt her mind caress his. "My forest glade is small, my Sanctuary is vulnerable. Ignorance and greed have permeated the minds of mankind. The warlords of the kingdoms surrounding our Empire are disrupting its harmony. I wish for you to help me heal and protect it. Will you do this for me?"

Follin's mind wandered back to his time in that same glade and of the wonders he experienced there in trance under her guidance.

"Of course, your will is mine to fulfill. It will be done if it is within my power."

"I have one other request. Eve has powers that need to be awakened. She may never discover these powers without Mage Hermes' help, and mine."

Slowly the High Priestess's image and fragrant, forest perfume faded, and Follin felt the chill of the night air. He could hear Eve's voice calling for him to join them for dinner.

When they had cleaned up after their meal, Alice pulled a piece of paper from her bodice. The paper was folded into many squares.

"What is this?" asked Follin as she handed it to him.

"The Emperor asked me to hand this to you when you agreed to join him. It's a map of your journey. This first picture here, see it? See that Pentacle, the circle with the star inside? It signifies the beginning. After we meet with The Emperor we will journey there, to my home, the Pentacles Kingdom."

Both Follin and Eve stared at the paper. It contained images. The first was a hand reaching out of a cloud, clasping a Pentacle. Below was a garden with white flowers. They looked like lilies, perfect in every way, as though crafted by a master artisan. Beyond the garden was a mountain range.

"Ready?" asked Alice.

"Now?" Follin and Eve asked in unison.

"Yes," replied Alice.

Follin looked to Eve, who nodded and went to pack their meagre belongings.

On her return Page Alice motioned for them to stand beside her. "Look closely, my dear friends. Look closely and walk with me through the garden gate. Come with me on this journey to the Emperor's castle in the foothills of those mountains, the mighty Hindamars." The Pentacles Page held their minds as she had been taught. The three left the humble cottage to find themselves standing before the tall, imposing walls of the Emperor's castle at the centre of the Tarot Empire.

Follin's meditation – Ace of Pentacles

Later that night as he was preparing for bed, Follin pulled from his pocket the sheet of paper that Alice had given him. He looked at the first picture, the one with the hand and a pentacle.

'That was the gateway we just went through,' he said to himself.

In his meditation, Follin sat on a hill overlooking the Pentacles Kingdom. Everywhere below he saw order in the fields and buildings, industrious workers plying their trades.

The word "Precision" came to his mind. 'How different from my life so far,' he thought.

He watched as a Pentacle circle appeared on the sun then floated down onto the land, rolling gently toward him up the hill. Light and a gentle warmth spread throughout the countryside. The scents of nectar-filled blossoms and rich, moist soil generated by the rolling Pentacle aroused Follin's awareness of the earth's vigour. Just as the Pentacle reached him it fell flat on the ground at his feet. Instinctively he stood upon it.

'This Pentacle is so grounding. It's as if my feet could sprout roots into the soil.'

He drew a deep breath. Light suffused his being, energizing him for the Pentacles sojourn ahead.

TWO OF PENTACLES

**Balance, to adapt in the face of hardship,
the secret of the 'change point'.**

Their first encounter with the Emperor was outside his castle walls under a starlit, night sky. The Emperor looked exactly as Follin remembered him: powerfully built and sitting astride his horse. He cantered over to them.

"Hail and well met, young Follin!" he thundered in his deep, powerful voice, "and to you, Eve, dear wife of my friend, you are most welcome. The Empress and I are excited that you have decided to accept our hospitality. I want you to know that while you are under my roof you are members of my family."

The richly dressed Emperor dismounted and walked over to his page. "Alice, please inform Mage Hermes that I wish to introduce him to Eve at supper." Handing his horse to one of his squires, the Emperor turned to Follin and Eve. He then embraced them warmly asking them to walk with him.

It was a cold evening and he intended to keep them out only for a short while. He escorted them through the castle gates and walked them into the keep.

"Follin, I remember meeting a lost youth some years ago. Today I see that he has grown into a young man with a charming and talented wife." The Emperor guided them up a flight of aged, stone stairs which brought them to a tall spire atop his castle. The walk was long and steep but he appeared no more fatigued than his young guests.

"I heard that you were seeking employment, Follin. Sir Cecil informed me of your excellent performance. I knew that I had made the right decision when we met for the first time and I took you to ride with me to view my Empire. After consideration with my wife, the Empress, Mage Hermes, High Priestess Hera and Sir Cecil, I have decided to invite you to join me to help me manage my vast Empire." This statement made Follin gasp. "Yes, I know we spoke of rulership and management when we met back then, but now I wish to do it properly, formally." He put his hand up to stop Follin from interrupting with questions. "I have need of youthful zeal as well as wise counsel, and I know you have both."

"Sire, I didn't know you knew Sir Cecil. My village is a long way away, in the Mystic Isles. It's often raided by the Wildlanders and some people consider us Wildlanders too."

"Sir Cecil served me well for many years. He is part Wildlander himself, a little like you. I was in need of his wild elemental magic then, as I am in need of yours now," replied the Emperor.

Follin shook his head in bewilderment, finally he asked, "Sire, but why do you need Eve, you don't even know her?"

"But I do know of her. Her father served me as a young man. His family and Eve's mother's family, have provided healers to my Kingdoms for many generations. Eve has a mix of both Mystic Isle and Wildlander blood, and her parents' healing skills are legendary. Sadly, war and plague have left Eve the last of her line, heir to their unique heritage. She holds the legacy of generations of healing wisdom in her blood. I did not want that lost to humanity." He looked at Eve and saw her eyes widen. The Emperor spoke to her directly.

"I'm sorry for your loss, Eve. If I had the power to stop warfare I would. What took your parents and your sister was beyond my control. You will both learn that sometimes we must accept the things we cannot change. Warfare, man's hatred and greed, are beyond our comprehension, and sadly, our control." He paused as he looked out beyond the castle walls. "Eve, the Wildlanders are being pulled from one faction to another. They have little order or structure which makes them vulnerable to being manipulated and used. I have no control over their lands, I have enough to do to manage my own Empire. The northern warlords' greed has now flooded into my Empire, my kingdoms suffer the Wildlander raids and they have sought to plunder our most sacred Sanctuary, the High Priestess's glade. I need you, and I need Follin, to assist in righting these wrongs."

Eve stood looking at the night sky. "What about my grandparents still hiding in the deep woods, Sire? They continue their healing, surely they could be brought here to help?"

"Yes, I did invite them to join me. Their loyalty to their family and their people was greater than their desire for the security of serving my Empire. They chose the path least travelled, the path of service to humanity in the worst of conditions. Sadly, they too have now passed beyond the lands of the living. I tried to protect them, but the soldiers of our enemy learned of their cabin hidden deep in the forest. I am very sorry. They asked that I accept you in their place. I have fulfilled my promise to them, in doing so I honour them. In turn, our Empire is honoured that you have accepted my invitation to join us here."

At that, Eve's mind whirled, without her husband's arms around her she would have fallen.

"Please, grieve for your loss, for tomorrow we have need of your courage and strength. The Empire is at risk and we believe that you both hold the keys to its salvation." The Emperor stretched his arms wide. They were now high above the castle and the Tarot Empire spread to the horizon. "My dear children, look, before you lies my Empire, the four Kingdoms. Embrace it with your eyes for tomorrow your journey to ensure its survival begins."

Within the hour, Alice, the Page of Pentacles, had them bathed and dressed ready to meet formally with the Emperor, the Empress and several of the castle staff. Most importantly, the Emperor wished them to speak with his Magician and alchemist, Mage Hermes.

Alice opened the door to the reception room then quietly left. She had already coached the lovers on how they should address their hosts. Follin bowed deeply and introduced his wife to the Empress.

"Your Majesty, Madam Empress, I am honoured to be back with you both once again. Thank you for inviting us to join you this evening. We are truly curious and excited to learn of our tasks." Follin stopped talking to bring his wife to stand by his side," and now I wish to introduce my beautiful wife, Eve."

"Eve, it is our honour that you have joined us. We want you to know that we are delighted to have you here and that you are now part of our family. All you need do is speak to any of our staff and they will do your bidding." The Empress now addressed her friend. "Follin, I see that you have grown in mind, body and spirit since your early days with us. Now please join us for refreshments."

The Empress petted one of the many cats parading around the room. In fact, there were cats and dogs everywhere in the castle and its grounds, or so it seemed to the young man. He could not quite remember if it was this crowded when he was here all those years ago.

The Empress asked Eve to sit beside her for the moment. She was curious about this young Mystic Isle woman with her bright eyes and inquisitive expression.

"My dear, please sit beside me. I would be delighted to talk with you." Follin brought Eve across with a knowing smile on his face. He recalled how he had felt overawed on his first visit with the Empress and was sure that Eve would be feeling much the same.

The Emperor had a jug of wine in one hand and was writing with his other. He finally looked up when his wife finished speaking.

"We have been honoured to be part of your journey, Follin, right from the beginning. We've proudly watched as you overcame the challenges set before you. We were all delighted when you returned home safely to your lover, Eve. We've had plans for young Eve since she was a child, too, but the intervening wars and plagues put our plans on hold, until today. To find you both together, at the exact right time, is a blessing for us and our empire."

Turning to Mage Hermes, the Emperor said, "Mage Hermes, would you please explain to our guests what we have planned for Eve?"

The aged alchemist, Mage Hermes, stood and introduced himself.

"Follin, since we last met I have travelled far and wide, in time and in space, as well as deep within the inner worlds, to find what is required in our time of need. Alas, there is always a fee for experience and wisdom, for which I have paid a heavy price. My journeys have aged me somewhat," he coughed as though a little embarrassed, "however my powers have increased."

Follin had been watching the Mage closely from the moment he heard him speaking softly with the Emperor. He could see that he had indeed aged.

The Mage was smiling as he stepped around the table and embraced his young friend. "My son, that day I last saw you was one of the brightest of my life. I look forward to preparing your talented and knowledgeable wife, Eve, and initiating her into the secrets along her path. We all have work to do, our Empire is in need of youth, courage and Mystic Isle magic - which you both hold within you." Mage Hermes stood before Eve, he embraced her as well. "And it is to you that I direct my next explanation."

All this time Eve was entranced by everyone, she even noticed the noble bearing of her husband when he was asked to present her. She marvelled at how respected her husband was by these powerful people.

"Eve, as the Emperor has explained, you come from a family of healers who have served our kingdom for many generations. Their legacy is in your spirit, your blood and your mind. This legacy enables you to understand the power of the plants we eat, the water we drink, the air we breathe and the sunlight that gives life to our world. Where Follin learned to walk among the archetypal giants of the Major Arcana, your own journey starts with me, just a wee giant. I shall do my best to educate you in the craft of alchemy and to awaken and tame your Mystic Isle magic." The Mage paused to catch his breath. The two Mystic Islanders noted how the aged Mage spoke softly and appeared easily fatigued.

"You will meet with other members of the Major Arcana, just as your husband did, but for a different purpose. In some ways, your path will be easier than Follin's, in other ways it will be much harder. Follin's father was a mage, though he had little time to teach his son his craft before he left on his own journey of healing. You will both participate in the secret initiations into the four Elements: Pentacles Earth; Swords Air; Cups Water; and Wands Fire. Unfortunately, you may be separated, physically, for some periods of time to allow you both to learn your lessons more thoroughly."

The small gathering went quiet as though waiting for someone to speak. At last the Emperor finished his writing and stood to ask the company to follow them into the feasting room to sit around the roaring fire. Follin found he had to compete with several cats and dogs for a seat close enough to feel the warmth from the hearth's flames.

"Eve?" the Emperor called softly. "It is our wish that you give yourself time to decide if this is what you want. I've asked my staff and my friends to provide every support and to answer every question you may have."

"Sire," said Eve, "I've already decided. I wish to begin immediately. I have but the one question."

The Emperor nodded for her to continue.

"If we fail in our quest, what will befall us? Will we be cast away only to be forced to start all over again, as paupers, in some strange and lonely village, in a land we don't know?"

The Empress put her hand on the Emperor's just as he began to speak. She spoke for them both.

"My dear daughter, we asked you here to spend the rest of your days with us regardless of your answer, or what may befall us all in the future. Although we know you won't fail the trials before you, no matter what happens there will always be a place at our table for you. This decision has been lifetimes in the making."

Eve and Follin turned to look at each other. Neither spoke, they were now even more confused.

The Empress continued. "My dear, though you are of age to have children of your own and participate as adults, to me you are as my own children. This is all new to you now, but the truth will be revealed, in time. Please trust us and your instincts."

At the end of their supper Mage Hermes spoke. "Eve, you will be working very closely with both myself and the High Priestess. We promise to be gentle but our time is brief and we have a lot to teach you. For now, we shall leave you in peace to talk and think about your quest together. We shall all meet again on the morrow." With that he stepped over to the young lovers and took their hands in his. Wishing their hosts 'good evening' he led them to their rooms.

"Alice?" the Mage called softly upon entering the palatial rooms the Mystic Islanders had been assigned. "Alice, are you here?" To Follin and Eve, the Mage whispered, "I bet she's fallen asleep. She's been up since before dawn and a soft, featherdown mattress is her personal weakness."

There came a sensuous groan from their bedroom. After some moments out walked Alice, still half asleep, her hair a mess.

"I'm awake, Mage Hermes," she answered. Suddenly she fully awoke and realised where she was. "I am so sorry! I just had your rooms made up and prepared… but the effort of magic and travel and everything… I just couldn't stay awake."

The young page stretched, yawning. Like a bear waking from hibernation, she smiled disarmingly at the three.

"It's fine, Alice," said Eve, "we've just come from discovering a little of why we're here, so we didn't need our bed, not until now that is." With a quick hug for the Mage and Alice, Eve eased past them and ran into the bedroom. "I've got the window side!"

Follin shook his head and smiled. "Thank you both for your kind welcome. I look forward to a good night's sleep and breakfast on the morrow. Perhaps I'll meet some old friends in my dreams tonight. See you in the morning."

Follin's meditation – Two of Pentacles

Follin sat quietly with the image of the Two of Pentacles in his mind. He saw a youth standing on one leg holding two pentacles in a figure of eight loop with two sailing ships on a stormy sea in the background.

Follin felt as though he was trying to steer a ship in a troubled sea. He worried if he should take this tack or that? Should he accept his quest? But what if Eve changed her mind? Or perhaps Eve should accept and not himself? He felt that they were being tossed about like the ships in the image.

Eventually Follin found himself on an isolated beach. He was alone, washed up by the tide. He sat and watched as the two sailing ships battled the waves in the distance. The winds had picked up and the ocean was restless.

Then a voice came into his mind. It was Hera, the High Priestess speaking so softly that he had to strain to listen against the roar of the sea. "Follin, remember your lessons during your sojourn amongst the Major Arcana."

She told him to calm his mind and that this would calm the seas. Follin began his slow, centred breathing and soon his mind was settled. To his amazement, the ocean, too, did settle.

"Find your state of internal peace and harmony and the outer world will match it," came the disembodied voice of the High Priestess.

"Whenever we embark on a new endeavour there is always initial resistance. There are always doubts, questions that you should have asked and deeds you should have done." At that, he found the figure 8 in his hands, turned on its side. Within each circle was a pentacle spinning in an endless loop. It was the magical symbol for infinity, a lemniscate. As one Pentacle went higher the other dropped, always in balance but fluid. Follin watched as the lemniscate in his hands twisted and writhed – alive.

"Follin what you are holding is the balance between actuality and possibility," Hera breathed softly into his mind.

Then Follin felt something shift within him. He realised that he had control of the balance of what is and what could be, that he was the one who controlled the 'point of change'. He was infinity and he could divine and control it. This was not just an image, it was life, and it was within him to use it, to bend it to his will – to adapt to change and life's fluctuations.

"Feel the 'change point'," Follin heard his own voice say inside his head. "If I put my mind to 'be' the change point I can tilt it forwards or backwards. I become the power to create my future. I can shift the balance within time and space, all I need to do is find that critical 'change point'."

"But what is the change point here?" Follin asked.

"Here, it is your moment of decision."

The lemniscate stopped spinning; it paused, hovering. In that moment Follin realised that had decided to accept his quest. His doubts, fears and uncertainties had disappeared.

"Well done, Follin," Hera's voice held a warmth that he recalled from their time together on his Major Arcana sojourn many years ago.

"But it has started spinning again," fretted Follin.

"And it will continue to spin its possibilities until your next decision," Hera replied.

As soon as Follin awoke he reached for his journal and wrote down the details of his meditation.

THREE OF PENTACLES
Teamwork, planning, competence, recognition.

As Follin fell into a deep sleep, Eve woke to a soothing light which appeared in the middle of her forehead. As she brought her mind to focus on the light she found herself in the High Priestess's forest glade, the Sanctuary. At the moment she saw her, Eve became transfixed by the High Priestess's beauty. Hera was tall, pale, almost translucent of skin and soft in manner. The image was fleeting and then faded, leaving just a glow, a glimmering shape.

The shape spoke to her. "My dear girl, I have brought you to my Sanctuary to invite you to learn women's sacred magic."

Eve was mesmerized by the archetype's melodious voice coming from her disembodied shadowy presence. She herself was still partly in her physical body and could feel an almost paralysing ecstasy as the Sanctuary's energy flowed into her.

"You're Hera, the High Priestess. Follin spoke of you a lot, he holds you in very high esteem," she said excitedly.

"My dear, Follin is a kind and loving person, but he is a male. He is yet to become whole, at which time he will truly appreciate my beauty and power. You are a woman, you will learn to know me organically, within your being. Follin has yet to learn to do that, this is not his time. He has much to accomplish before he can be initiated into our mysteries. He has touched upon my gifts - but only lightly. It is you I want and need."

The High Priestess put a glowing hand out to the young woman and touched her in the middle of the forehead. Immediately Eve was fully in the Sanctuary glade itself.

"Madam, am I really here? I mean, am I really in your Sanctuary?" Eve asked, her eyes darting everywhere trying to take it all in.

"Yes, you certainly are. I've brought you here so that you can better understand what I am about to teach you while you are in your dream body. If you were to wake up now you would wake up in your own bed, next to your husband. You will learn to experience my Sanctuary in two ways: like this, in your dream body while you are asleep or meditating; and by visiting here physically, though that is very difficult for my Sanctuary is well hidden." Hera paused to let this information sink in.

"With practice you will be able to access my Sanctuary by travelling in either form, physical or astral. Tonight I have brought you here to introduce you to our Empire's hidden magic, women's magic. Women have powers men don't understand and the Sanctuary harbours one form of magic that binds our Tarot Empire to the land itself. The highest male initiates can only touch upon these powers." Again Hera stopped to let Eve absorb this information.

"The feminine is power itself. Males assist in conception but it is women who take their sperm to create the matter of life itself."

Eve stood watching the story of life unfold as the High Priestess spoke in pictures, feelings and words.

"I know this to be true, we gestate the baby and give birth, but aren't men more powerful than women? Aren't they our protectors?" asked Eve.

The High Priestess's throaty laughter floated through the glade. "My dear daughter, we create and men protect our creations. We are programmed to nest while men are programmed to protect our nest. That's just nature's way. No, men are not more powerful than women."

It was difficult for Eve to stay in this altered state of consciousness, she felt fatigue creeping through her body. The High Priestess had completed her lesson for this evening and watched, a smile spreading across her face.

"The seeds I planted in Follin seven years ago have finally grown to maturity. The fruit is almost ready for the picking. My dear Eve, sleep now, your journey through the Tarot's elemental Kingdoms has just begun."

———

"Follin?" called Eve as she stepped out of the bathtub, "did you know that women are more powerful than men?"

Follin was looking through their kitchen window enjoying the wonderful view across the valley and up into the snow-capped Hindamar Mountains.

"Huh? What are you talking about? Men are heaps stronger than women."

"No," replied Eve, "that's not what I meant. Women have powers that men don't."

"Oh, sure, I knew that. Men can't make children," he replied knowingly, "why?"

"I met with the High Priestess last night, in her Sanctuary, and she spoke to me about women's powers."

Follin stopped his daydreaming and walked to the bathroom door. "You were with Hera, in her Sanctuary last night?" He was incredulous.

"Yes, she took me while I was dreaming. She's beautiful, no wonder you like her," said Eve. Part of her face reflected her bewilderment and part a wistfulness that she herself was not as beautiful as the High Priestess.

Follin intuited Eve's doubts. "I never saw her as beautiful in that way, Eve. In fact, I rarely saw her in real life at all. I met her in my dreams, and I could hear her voice inside my head."

"She's teaching me things," said Eve, a little relieved, as she stepped from the bath, a towel loosely draped around her lithe body. "This is all so confusing, though. How did I ever get caught up in this weird adventure of yours?"

Follin laughed as he grabbed her by the waist and swung her around, her towel falling to the floor.

There came a knock on the door. It was Alice, calling to announce that breakfast was served and they were expected in the dining room. Eve quickly covered herself and opened the door, Alice stepped back apace.

"Mistress, I am your servant, but I don't need to join you in your boudoir with your husband quite undressed as you are," Alice blushed. "Please, allow me to dress you and then we can be on our way. In future I will arrive and wake you, then help you dress and escort you both to breakfast. The Emperor and Empress are most exact when it comes to meal times." Alice blushed once again when Eve led her into their bedroom letting her towel drop to the floor.

When she saw Alice blush a deeper hue of red, Eve quickly drew her towel back around her body.

"I'm sorry, Alice, I wasn't sure if people are supposed to be naked when they get dressed by their page. It's just that everything is so new, so strange and I'm at a loss to know what is expected of us. We depend on your common sense and guidance in the ways of the court," she said covering her own embarrassment.

This was exactly what she needed to say to Alice. The Page of Pentacles had only one way of coping with change, and that was by sticking to what she knew best: routines and common sense. Any deviation from the norm would put her head into a spin, then she would become confused and distressed.

"Mistress Eve, that's a deal. I'll set the routines and remind you every day until you remember them. It's just that you are so beautiful and I wasn't prepared for, you know, so much skin." Alice smiled and they both started to giggle, it relieved the tension. Her dilemma was now resolved and the Page felt back on firm ground.

At breakfast, the Emperor asked Follin to join him on a tour of his kingdom. He turned to Eve and asked if she was ready to take on her training for the day.

"Sire, not only am I ready but I'm delighted now that I've met the High Priestess. I think I'm starting to understand why we're here." She looked at the Empress who smiled back, in a knowing, feminine way. Like co-conspirators, they smiled behind their hands.

"Ah, I see, so now the female fraternity are ganging up on us weak and feeble menfolk?" He laughed out loud. Follin looked at them quizzically.

The Empress spoke to ease his confusion. "Today, Eve will start her lessons with Mage Hermes who will provide support and guidance along with myself and High Priestess Hera. Mage Hermes will also assist you with your journey. My husband will help but, alas, these are tough times and he is often busy on urgent matters for the safety and security of our Empire. Your learning will pass to the Pentacles Kingdom. You have already met their Page, the delightful Alice. Now relax and eat your breakfast. Afterwards, Follin, you'll be attending the Emperor while Mage Hermes will escort you, Eve, to show you around the castle and begin your lessons in the Empire's magic."

The Emperor sat astride his stallion, a powerful beast. Beside him waited his favourite hunting dog looking forward to his daily exercise. Follin mounted the same horse he had ridden almost seven years ago.

"Son, things are not as peaceful as they were when last you visited us. The many kingdoms of the wild lands surrounding our Empire are looking upon us with greedy eyes, but, sadly, the power that protects our land is waning. We need both you and Eve to do your utmost to help us ensure the safety of our Empire and our four Tarot Kingdoms."

At that Follin's eyes went wide. "Sire, that's quite a task! What can we do? We're only two little people. I don't even have a sword or a weapon of any kind."

"I believe the High Priestess called upon you to help her secure her Sanctuary? You know that the Sanctuary is the centre of our universe. We are an extension of that magical glade and thus we endeavour to protect it. The Empire and Sanctuary are one. Without the Sanctuary we would cease to exist on this beautiful planet. There are many other planes of existence, but this one, well, this has so many more… opportunities," explained the Emperor.

When Follin tried to ask for more information on this subject, the Emperor put his finger to his lips to indicate silence. He put his horse into a gallop and they raced across the hills towards a gap in the valley. They rode into the foothills of the mountain ranges surrounding the Emperor's castle. For Follin, who had had little opportunity to ride, a gallop with the Emperor was more frightening than thrilling. As they eventually slowed to walk their now tired horses, the Emperor began speaking once more.

"Follin, the Empire is created from four elements, the Tarot Elemental Kingdoms. If we lose a single one of them we cease to exist. These four Kingdoms surround this castle and the High Priestess's Sanctuary. We must ensure they survive for our own survival. If we lose one we lose them all."

It was too much for Follin to grasp. The Emperor pushed his horse forwards, finally dismounting on a peak overlooking the four Tarot Empire Kingdoms.

"There, look, see that river? If you had the eyes of an eagle you would see the ocean beyond. That marks the boundary of the Cups Kingdom, the Kingdom of water. The mountain range you see north of us marks the border of the Pentacles Kingdom, the Kingdom of earth and rock. You will be spending time with them very soon. The King of Pentacles is one of my favourites, a solid, practical, down-to-earth man. He asked that he be the first to teach you his elemental magic." The Emperor remounted and together they rode for another hour to the other side of the ridge. There they saw a spire of smoke from a volcanic mountain peak.

"In that direction is the Wands Kingdom. They rule fire and, although I sometimes despair at their party loving, thrill seeking ways, I rejoice in their creative spirit. In that direction lies the Swords Kingdom with its many forests and grassy plains which seem to go on forever. The Swords rule air and the intellect. They wanted to be the first to train you but I thought the grounding you'll learn with the Pentacles would be most appropriate at this stage of your journey."

It was an amazing sight: mountains, valleys, forests, rivers and a smoking volcano. But it would take some time for Follin to process its enormity.

"I like Alice, she told us that she's of Pentacles royalty. I'd feel most comfortable being with her Pentacles people first, I think," offered Follin as he pondered the vast scale of the Empire and its Kingdoms.

While Follin was with the Emperor, Eve was sitting with Mage Hermes watching him prepare a bed of soil for his sprouted garlic.

"Some soils have every quality necessary to nurture the plant you want to grow, while other soils have different or very few properties," he explained. "There is magic in soil, ancient magic that goes back beyond human time. This soil was brought down from the side of the volcano in the Wands Kingdom. It contains just about every mineral a plant needs to flourish. We now honour the garlic and plant each clove above a small handful of crushed eggshells."

The Mage placed the eggshells into the small holes drilled into the freshly turned earth. He added a fine layer of reddish soil and placed the green-tipped garlic cloves above it. Lastly, he filled the holes with more soil, then gently patted it down smooth.

"So, every plant needs special soil, like the volcanic soil of the Wands people, plus eggshells?" Eve asked.

"Every plant has specific needs, specific foods which it will feed upon. Garlic just so happens to like eggshells. Celery, on the other hand, likes friendship. We would plant them next to tomatoes or beans. They get lonely and prefer a friend other than their own species. Much like a goat and sheep, they enjoy their own kind but for some reason they also enjoy the company of other species. Even dogs and cats thrive alongside another species such as humans."

The Mage next took Eve to the enormous compost bins outside the kitchens.

"Nothing is wasted, Eve, even dead animals can be buried beneath certain plants to enhance their growth and their healing powers. And then there are the worms, our favourite gardeners." He dug his fingers into the compost bin and lifted a handful of wriggling worms for Eve to see. "These little creatures do most of the work for us. They turn our food scraps into nutrients for our plants. They hold a certain magic to enhance plant life. Everything we might think of as waste is actually an opportunity to create life and vitality."

Eve took a handful of compost and studied the worms. She noted that some were large, some small and some barely visible.

"If you just sit down here I'll show you a secret." The Mage carefully brushed all but a tiny pile of compost from his hand. All that was left were three tiny eggs. "See these little balls, they're eggs, worm eggs. These will hatch just like chickens and a dozen baby worms will birth ready to do your work for you. This is the magic of compost and the magic of feeding our kitchen waste to the workers who make our gardens a haven for our health."

"I know about worms but I didn't know they laid eggs, and I've always put our food scraps on our vegetable garden. Is that good enough?" asked Eve.

"Burying our scraps makes it easier for the worms to do their magic. We then add compost to our healing plants to increase their potency." The Mage took Eve's hand in his and walked her into the kitchen where the hustle and bustle of so many staff made her head spin. He went straight to the kitchen waste bin and pulled out a bucket of scraps.

"This is your first task, turn this into food for your parsley, angelica and lemon balm. Walk me through what you are doing and why," requested Hermes as he sat carefully on a log beside his own herb garden.

By this time some of the kitchen staff were watching and asked Eve what she was doing. They knew that Eve and Follin had arrived from the Mystic Isle and were curious.

"I'm making compost for our plants," replied Eve to the various queries from the staff.

"Aye, that be simple 'nuff m'lady, just throw it on't ground and up will spring yon carrot. Them tops be ready for planting, if 'yer careful 'nuff," said one aged kitchen hand, busy shifting a bag of flour fresh from the mill.

"Why thank you, sir, I shall give that a try, too," said Eve, delighted that the Emperor's staff were just as prepared to help as the Mage himself.

"So now you know another secret, some plants don't need seeds or bulbs, some can be cut and planted immediately for another crop," added the Mage, shifting his bulk to sit more comfortably on the log's uneven surface.

"I've grown carrots and turnips like this before. My father taught me when I was a child. It certainly speeds things up, but not all of them survive," answered Eve.

"I know, Eve, this method has been around for aeons, but there's a reason I want you to start from the beginning. I want you to know exactly what and why from a magician's perspective. Now let's work on your composting. Start your garden bed over there, on virgin ground, and let's see how you go," instructed the Mage, delighted to have such an astute student.

The lessons progressed each day and Eve enjoyed every second. Some things she already knew and some she did not. All in all, just knowing that what she had been doing all her life was correct, made the lessons so much more enjoyable.

Follin, on the other hand, struggled. His lessons covered the history of the Kingdoms and the current political situation - and he was not in the least bit interested. He learned by 'doing', not by 'listening'.

Follin recalled the many times in school when he was called upon to answer a question in class and everyone laughed at him because he could not remember a thing. The teacher would then flog him mercilessly. The beatings were to no avail. His memory was worse after a beating – and, thus, he remained the class fool. This memory now flooded his mind and body until the Emperor told him that, if he did not learn the history of the Empire, he was putting everyone's lives at risk.

Follin's eyes widened and he asked, "Do you mean that we could all disappear? Eve and me as well?"

"Yes, that's right. We are bound to the Sanctuary. If it dies we no longer exist on this planet. The Sanctuary is bound by the balance between the four Tarot Kingdoms. Knowing the history of our Empire, its four Kingdoms and the Wildlands beyond, plus the political landscape within and beyond our homes is critical to a ruler – and to his advisers. If one of our Kingdoms is compromised by a poor choice of trade or even of marriage, it could put the Sanctuary out of balance, which compromises the Sanctuary's integrity. It wouldn't take long before our entire social and ecological system was in danger of destruction. Instability and disharmony in our Empire is real my son. It's very real and, sadly, very close." The Emperor sat on a rock overlooking the mountain ranges which formed part of the Pentacles Kingdom.

"I don't want to put you and your wife under pressure but we need you to study hard. Fortunately, I have a guest arriving tomorrow who may be able to speed things up. Don't stress, stay focused and use the skills the High Priestess and my wife, the Empress, taught you while you were on your journey through the Major Arcana."

The following morning they woke to a bright blue, cloudless sky. When Eve went off with Mage Hermes, Follin was introduced to the Emperor's guest, Sir Dale, a tall, angular Knight of Pentacles, a warrior of renown.

He was visiting his cousins and friends in the Emperor's court The Emperor had requested that he take Follin on, temporarily, as a squire.

As one of the knight's three squires, Follin felt uncomfortably out of his depth. He knew nothing of how a squire should behave and nothing about swordplay, armour or caring for a knight's horse and equipment.

"You're damn useless, Follin," exclaimed Mavor, the head squire, watching Follin fumble with the knight's saddle. "We'll have to do most of the work ourselves while you fluff around making mistakes. Or, worse still, crying that your arms are sore and your hands cracked and bleeding." He turned to his number two, Allen, snickering beside with him.

"I've been ordered to teach you how to serve our lord, properly, as a squire should. Sir Dale is a hero in our kingdom, a real hero, not just the romantic ones the Swords and Cups sing about. He's saved our Kingdom single handed, as well as successfully leading our armies against the Wildlanders, countless times. He needs the best service and we're it. I don't expect you'll last very long."

Mavor roughly grabbed at Follin's hands and held them up. "Allen, look at his hands, they're soft like a baby's bottom." The two squires roared with laughter. "Now get to the stables and muck out the mess there. I'll work you till you bleed, and don't think you can whine to our Master, he doesn't need a whining sop to babysit for the Emperor."

Follin felt miserable, humiliated and useless. His head dropped as he followed the older youths to the stables. Mavor grabbed a three-pronged, wooden fork and threw it at him.

"We'll be back in an hour. If these stalls aren't mucked out properly, then we'll have to show you how we treat lazy asses in the vale," called Allen over his shoulder. They left Follin alone to get on with his task.

It appeared easy enough, raking and forking the manure and straw into piles, then shoveling them into a wheelbarrow to dump into the compost bins outside. But, after a while, Follin's back hurt, then his hands started to crack and bleed in the cold, dry air. The squires did not return until it was time for lunch, but Follin had only been able to clean out half the stables.

Mavor called his partner over and they both looked inside. Sir Dale had four horses but only two stalls were presentable. Follin was terrified. He had worked as hard as his exhausted body could. Unused to this style and method of work he was ready to collapse.

"Well, no lunch for you, worm, you've hardly done an hour's work," Mavor grunted, then winked at Allen. Pretending to leave, they suddenly swung around and leapt on Follin, knocking him to the ground. "You've made us look bad, worm, you deserve what you get. Come on, Allen, let's show this worthless islander what we do to bludgers and slackers."

The two squires dragged Follin by the feet to the water trough where they held his head under the water until he stopped struggling. They then let him up for air. Follin was only semiconscious so they revived him with a sharp slap to his face.

"You're pathetic! We've just started and already you've given up! It looks like we'll have to demonstrate what we do with losers who give up too easily." The boys then stripped him naked and threw him into the filthiest stall. Follin slipped and fell among the horse droppings and urine soaked straw. The two squires then prodded him with the pitchfork. The wicked, sharp points drew blood each time they touched his pale skin.

Mavor and Allen left him there to finish the final two stalls. Follin had no strength even to get up. He just curled into a ball on the stable floor and sobbed in despair.

Follin was still struggling to finish his tasks when the squires returned at sundown and sent him back to his rooms. They threatened that if he did not pull his weight tomorrow they would do the same again.

"Don't even pretend to yourself that Sir Dale will want you as a squire. He needs squires who know how to look after a knight properly, and you,

you're just a useless waste of space." Allen shouted at Follin's bloodied and bruised back.

Follin was completely exhausted. He did not attend dinner nor supper, and his wife finally found him asleep in the bathtub. Eve was horrified at what she saw. She did not know what to do so she raced off to find Page Alice. Recognising the urgency in Eve's voice Alice followed her back to their rooms.

"Those brutes!" she said when she saw Follin's bleeding hands, the bruises and cuts to his skin. Alice averted her eyes as best she could as the two girls pulled him, barely conscious, from the bath and dressed his wounds.

"I'm going to have a word with Sir Dale, he's an honourable man, a warrior through and through. If he knew what his squires did he'd have stepped in and stopped them straight away. The rotten mongrels!" Alice swore softly.

Eve was silent as she slowly spoonfed her exhausted, miserable husband with a bowl of broth she brought back from the kitchen.

"He's a hard worker, I'll give him that, but whatever it was he had to do today must have broken him. And those squires have surely ill-treated him. I don't mind hard work, but bullying, I'll never tolerate. Tomorrow I'm going down to the stables to have words with them." Eve finally spoke her mind. Her voice was hard, it quivered with suppressed rage and pain.

Alice helped her dress Follin in his nightclothes and put him to bed. Together the girls pulled up his blankets and left him alone.

Finally Alice spoke. "Eve, if you don't mind, I think I'm the best one to deal with this. I know Sir Dale, he's my cousin, we've always gotten along well. He'll listen to me. If you say anything he'll think you're just a meddling wife."

"Thanks, Alice, I think I'm a bit too emotional at the moment to think straight." Eve's voice was soft, it sounded like she was ready to collapse herself. Covering her face with her hands she sobbed, "I'm afraid that we've made the wrong decision in coming here. We should have stayed in Saoirse village. At least we were happy there."

The following morning Follin was up well before dawn and mucking out the stables. No one else was about. Eve had tried to stop him but he had brushed her aside. The depth of his humiliation drove him to work the shame from his memory. He had been in this place before. He clearly recalled those years of shame struggling to hold onto what little pride he had when forced to sit in the fool's chair at school.

Sir Dale arrived midmorning. The two squires were with him.

"Follin, I see you've cleaned my stables, and a damn fine job you've done too. But come over here and stand by me. I want to talk about what I have planned for you." Follin was near collapse anyway so this was a welcome respite.

The knight felt Follin's biceps and his shoulders and poked and prodded his body here and there. He pretended not to notice the blood-soaked rags which Follin had wrapped around his bleeding hands so that he could grip the wooden, three-pronged fork.

"Just as I thought. You're wasted mucking out stables." Turning to Mavor he said, "You will continue with your tasks, leave Follin to me."

The Pentacles Knight paused to look intently at his two squires. "Is that clear?" He continued to stare them in the eye until they nodded and left. Follin had no idea that Alice had spoken to her cousin about the squire's mistreatment of him.

That evening when he returned to their rooms he called out to his wife. "Eve, guess what? Tomorrow we'll be going with Sir Dale to the Pentacles Kingdom. I'm to learn swordsmithing, or blademaking or something like that. He said that if I study hard I might be allowed to forge my own sword."

"I know," replied Eve, a twinkle in her eye. "Mage Hermes told me. He said that I'm going to learn more about the craft of healing and working with Pentacles magic. Mage Hermes said I needed to go to the Kingdom of the Pentacles where I'll learn more about soils, rocks and earth magic."

Eve instinctively reached for her husband's cut and swollen hands. She began to gently rub them with a healing balm The Magician had given her earlier that day.

The lovers were both in a good mood that night when they attended the common room for their meal. It was here that the two Mystic Islanders felt most relaxed. They enjoyed mixing with the household staff, more so than with the courtiers in the formal dining room.

Page Alice was there. "Sir Dale said I'm to come along with you to the Pentacles Kingdom, my home. I'll be your maidservant, Eve. He said it was time I learned how to tame a mistress from the wilds." She was so excited she could not stop giggling.

The three of them spent hours with the rest of the staff discussing topics as diverse as the failing energy of the High Priestess's Sanctuary and the price of hops for their beer brewing.

The Emperor and Empress joined them after dinner, freely chatting and engaging with their guests. It was a relaxing and fun time for the entire household staff and their young guests.

Follin understood only too well that his time in the Empire would not be easy. Although he was a favoured guest of the Emperor and Empress, he certainly would not be given an easy passage through his initiations. He had survived yesterday and today, but would he survive tomorrow? His main aim at this stage was to show he could perform as well as anyone at whatever task was handed him. He felt that he needed to prove he was not a quitter.

By the time they were ready to leave on their trek to the Pentacles Kingdom both Follin and Eve had begun their apprenticeships. They had passed through the initial stages of resistance and fear of change and knew that their quest warranted their very best effort.

Follin's meditation – Three of Pentacles

Follin sat up late on their last night in the Emperor's castle and studied the third picture. It was a stone mason working at his craft. In the image it appeared that the craftsman's work was being appraised by two well-dressed guildsmen. Perhaps they were masters of their craft? Follin was not sure.

'That's me,' he realised. 'I try my hardest but I'm fearful that someone will notice all the mistakes I make. I guess it means I should just do the best I can despite my fear of being judged. I need to remind myself to stay focused, that the very act of working to my best ability will be its own reward.'

But then Follin had another thought. 'Maybe the two guildsmen are listening to me explain what I have done and why. Maybe they value what I've done?'

He was still smiling contentedly as he entered his notes in his journal, then prepared for bed.

FOUR OF PENTACLES

Possessiveness, control, selfishness, arrogance breeds stagnation.

The poise and conduct of the Pentacles men-at-arms and cavalry made for a fine parade as they escorted the wagon train out of the Emperor's castle. They progressed carefully along the rough, forested track into the Pentacles Kingdom. The orderly line of horsemen and soldiers was perfection itself. The men-at-arms marched to the beat of a single drummer who tapped out a rhythm which set the soldiers singing martial songs, interspersed with songs of love, happiness and the rewards of a job well done.

The trek north to the Pentacles castle, nestled deep among the Hindamar Mountain foothills, took more than a week. The journey was always considered quite treacherous, so the soldiers and wagoneers were constantly on the alert for danger.

Follin rode with Mavor and Allen, their snide remarks and black looks suggested something had transpired between themselves and their master, Sir Dale. It did not bother him too much, but he felt a sense of rejection and loneliness.

Eve, though, was having the time of her life. She sat at the front of the wagon with the white-haired wagoneer, old Frailbones. He was of medium build but his powerful frame and clear, intense gaze, belied his name.

She was delighted to be back in the forest again. The girl from the Mystic Isle knew the names of most of the trees, shrubs and the herbs they passed, and what she did not recognise she asked her companion.

When she could she sang along with the soldiers and she laughed when they did a skip-step to the changes in rhythm, all orchestrated by the flamboyant drummer.

Eve kept up a constant conversation with her companion but every now and then she was interrupted by a query directed from behind her. Alice, and others of the Pentacles court, preferred to stay and chatter inside the warm wagon. The girls huddled inside were curious and kept asking Eve about what she was doing with High Priestess Hera and Mage Hermes. They had heard snippets from the other court members while at the Emperor's castle, but that only increased their desire to know more.

Until her reunion with Follin, Eve had lived a quiet and simple life, even during the turbulent war years. Despite her skills as a healer, she was socially ill-equipped for the sudden move to the court of the Emperor of the Four Tarot Kingdoms. She went from a nobody to a somebody in what was a whirlwind of excitement. Now everyone wanted to know her and sought out her friendship. She was treated as someone special. Eve liked her unaccustomed celebrity status; in fact, she liked it too much.

The Mystic Isle girl enjoyed teasing the girls. She was not going to give away any secrets nor was she about to share her knowledge with them.

In her eyes, studying under Mage Hermes and the High Priestess gave her a position of superiority.

"Eve, why don't you tell us about Mage Hermes? He's such a nice old man but so secretive. What is he really like? Come on, you never tell us anything," called Alice from the tiny wagon window. The court girls' cries sounded like a chorus behind her.

But Eve was adamant, she enjoyed her position of superiority and played on it. "All in due time, ladies, all in due time. Maybe tomorrow night, or when we arrive at the castle. Or… maybe the night after, that might be better, when I'm not so tired…"

Old Frailbones could not help but overhear their conversations. He noted how Eve teased the girls of the court and he was not impressed.

"Missus Eve, begging yer pardon fer me saying so, but why don't you tell the wee lasses a bit of what thee has seen and learned? It won't hurt none, and it might make them feel a wee bit special too."

Eve swung her head around to look at Alice through the window. She then turned to Frailbones considering her response.

"I've earned the right to study with the magicians, these courtly girls are just silly little things who wouldn't understand what I said anyway. Why should I tell them anything?" she said with a toss of her head sending her long, blond hair out of her eyes. Even as she spoke, Eve sensed a sliver of doubt: had she really earned that right?

"Now lass, don't be too hoity-toity with those you think beneath thee. They didn't have your opportunities in life nor are they talented like thee. They be nice girls and thee nay want them or anyone in our kingdom thinking thee too haughty to talk to." The old man kept his eyes on the path and deliberately did not look at Eve as he spoke, but he glanced at her as he ended his lecture. "Pride comes a'fore a fall, me pretty young lass, 'tis best to make a friend by being a friend."

"I've got more important things to do than make friends, Frailbones. Why do I need these girls as friends anyway? My friends are the Emperor's magicians," she said, trying to sound mature and wise.

Suddenly it occurred to her that she was acting rudely, especially to her friend, Alice, who, she reminded herself, had been so kind to her. Eve felt herself blush at Frailbones's gentle scolding and she dropped her face so he would not notice.

"Sometimes a friend be low as be high, me lass. When we stop for lunch I think it wise for thee to make thy peace with the lasses. They're fascinated by you Mystic Islanders. We folk of the Pentacles make honourable allies, we stick to our friends through thick and thin. Aye, a Pentacles friend gained, be a friend fer life." The two stopped talking as they neared a clearing where the cooks were busy preparing lunch.

While the small force of men-at-arms was preparing for their midday meal, Sir Dale sent his three squires forward to scout the path ahead. As soon as they were out of sight, Mavor called out to Follin, riding behind them.

"You gutless worm! Can't fight your own fights? Sir Dale told us off for initiating you into your squireship. He said we weren't to touch a hair on your precious head, we have to treat you with respect! What lies did you tell him?" He screwed up his face and shouted disgustedly, "Huh! You know nothing of warfare, you don't know a damn thing about swords; how to polish one; how to sharpen or even how to wield one. If it comes to a fight we ain't going to rescue you, Follin. You're just a stupid fool and if you want anything from us you'll have to squirm in the dirt like the islander worm that you are and beg for it."

Mavor looked across to Allen, and laughed. "You'll never learn our fighting tricks and skills, never. We've earned it the hard way. Since you're Sir Dale's pet, his golden-haired boy, you'll have to ask him what to do, if you dare. You'll be the fool you've always been without that learning. You should have kept your mouth shut and not crossed us."

Follin looked at them and intuited that they would not have taught him anything anyway. He was not one of them, a Pentacles. He was an outsider, a Mystic Islander, a nobody to them, a freak. The older squire spurred his horse and galloped ahead. Allen joined him, leaving Follin alone.

Only a few minutes had passed when he saw Allen and Mavor galloping back towards him. They both wore an expression of shock and fear as they skidded their horses to a halt.

"Follin, get back to the wagon train! Tell Sir Dale that there's a foot patrol of Wildlanders ahead. We'll stand-to here. If they approach we'll do what we can to hold them up a bit, then we'll fall back to the wagons. Now go!"

Follin spun his horse around awkwardly and galloped as best he could without falling off. As he reached the Pentacles campsite he cried out the news to the first soldiers he came to. Immediately a well-practised defensive perimeter sprang into existence.

Captain Bleecher yelled for his men-at-arms. They dropped what they were doing, raced for their weapons then stood in ordered rows, ready for his command. The girls and other members of the knight's household began packing up their foodstuffs and loaded their wagons. Although everything was done at speed, no one panicked. The first platoon of men-at-arms marched out with Captain Bleecher in the lead within moments.

An armed guard remained behind. Follin noticed Frailbones grab a bow and stand by his wagon. He had an arrow nocked ready on the string.

"Follin, to me!" called Sir Dale as he grabbed his armour and indicated for Follin to assist him. "What manner of weapon can you wield? Bow, sword, knife, slingshot?"

Follin was raised in Saoirse, a small village on the edge of the great forests of the Mystic Isle. As the eldest son he had spent most of his childhood in the forests hunting food for his family.

"Sire, I can use a hunting bow."

"Good. Sergeant Rollin, give the boy a bow and a quiver of arrows." He turned back to his new squire as he shrugged on his armour. He grunted, "If you can do justice to the bow you'll be worth your weight in gold this day." He paused briefly. "Have you ever killed a man?"

Follin was shocked. He had not thought of killing anyone before this.

"Sire, I've never killed anything larger than a rabbit, but I'm not afraid to protect my friends and family." Follin yanked the last of Sir Dale's armour buckles tight. "I will kill if I need to."

The Pentacles Knight did not hesitate. "Good, because I can hear fighting ahead. Just remember, archers are vulnerable in close-quarter fighting. Now help me mount." Sir Dale motioned to his cavalrymen and they were off. Follin soon followed.

As they rounded the bend they saw Mavor and Allen, swords in hand, fending off a half-dozen enemy soldiers. The cries of battle sounded loud in the forest gloom. The squire's horses pranced and kicked as the two flashed their swords but they only managed to inflict minor wounds. Skillfully the squires worked together to keep their enemy at bay, wheeling and turning their horses in a series of complicated maneuvers.

"Mavor! Where are the rest of the enemy?" called Captain Bleecher, leading his men at a run towards the fight.

Mavor panted his reply as he pulled at his horse's reins to avoid the desperate thrust of a Wildlander's spear point. "In the forest, trying to get around us, this is but a part." He grunted loudly once more, swinging his blade at the head of an opponent. "We saw perhaps twenty enemy but there will be more."

Realising they were outnumbered, the small band of Wildlanders turned and fled into the forest.

"Hold!" bellowed Captain Bleecher to his troops who were keen to pursue the fleeing enemy.

Mavor and Allen rejoined Sir Dale as he called to his men-at-arms: "Squad one, to the right and skirmish one hundred metres. Squad two, the same on the left flank. Send runners to report when you have cleared the area. Follin, gallop forward along the road. Scout ahead two hundred metres. Watch your flanks and report back what you see."

Follin had to manage his bow, a quiver of arrows and his horse, all at once and without falling off. He slipped in his saddle and almost fell several times. As he passed Mavor and Allen he noticed their grim faces were focused on the bushes on both sides of the track ignoring him completely.

At almost two hundred metres Follin's horse veered off the road into the forest. It stopped suddenly and Follin fell off. He landed awkwardly on his bow and it snapped. The horse skittered a few feet away then stood, as it had been trained to do. All was quiet and the gloom of the unfamiliar forest intimidating. The pine needles prickled his nose as he lay there, face down, momentarily stunned and defenceless.

Follin managed to get to his feet shakily. *'Earth yourself, as I taught you,'* he heard The Empress's voice. As he calmed and centred himself, he could feel energy flow down his legs, through the soles of his feet to sink deep below the forest floor. He sensed the roots of the trees around him drawing water, nutrients and life force into their being. When it reached the branches Follin could feel what the trees around him felt: the Wildlanders were perched in the trees and there was movement as they crept along the forest floor.

Enemy, there were enemy here, hidden. Some were archers, watching him, and he knew these would kill. They were not interested in him, though, they wanted Sir Dale and his wagons.

'They're more hungry than savage. They're just people, just like me,' he thought. *'They want me to report back that there is no one ahead so they can ambush us.'*

Follin felt something else, the soul of the forest itself. It spoke to him in sensations describing the danger hidden within its branches and undergrowth. Follin could feel the power of the forest. He recognised it as part of Pan; whose gift he had experienced many years ago when the Angel Temperance took him to Pan's cave. Drawing on Pan's earth magic, Follin sought the change point. With a twist of his life force he urged the forest to put terror into the hearts of the enemy and to give his own people safe passage.

Within moments Follin could hear branches snapping and saw movement as Wildlanders scrambled out onto the road screaming of the horrors in the forest.

Remembering his orders, Follin remounted and galloped back to his Knight to report.

"Sir Dale, the forest hid more of the enemy. I asked the trees to frighten them. They're now running away." The Knight saw that his new squire was not being proudful nor seeking praise. He had presented his report clearly and factually, then withdrawn.

"You evoked earth magic?" Sir Dale barked impatiently.

Follin was bewildered, so he just nodded, waiting for the rebuke.

"Hmm, I thought only Pentacles Masters had that power..." mused the Knight rubbing his forehead where the rim of his helmet irritated his skin.

"I don't know, Sire."

"Nicely done, Follin, nicely done." Sir Dale looked around at his men, checking to see that they were all present, then motioned them back to the campsite.

———

There were no more interruptions to their trip. For the remainder of the journey Mavor and Allen kept their distance. After hearing what Follin had done they decided it best to avoid a confrontation with him. What Follin could do frightened them.

At nightfall a few days later their ordered lines arrived at the Pentacles castle.

Follin's meditation – Four of Pentacles

The image showed a king, or royalty of some description, hoarding his treasure.

'I wonder what that means?' Follin said to himself as he sank deeper into trance. As he slid into his special place, the hermit's cottage, Follin found himself sitting in the sunshine with The Hierophant beside him.

"Son, it has been a while since we spoke and I see that you have come a long way. You now have a wife and the Tarot Empire has need of your Mystic Isle ways," *said The Hierophant.*

"Hail, Master Hierophant, yes, it has been a while since we last met. As you can see I still have puzzles to solve and this one eludes me." *Follin showed The Hierophant his picture.* "Does this mean we should control what we have? Perhaps it represents responsibility? Or is it greed and a failure to recognise the gifts that accompany sharing?"

"These are good questions. Let us enter the image and ask the fellow shall we?" suggested The Hierophant as he examined the picture. In the next moment the King of Pentacles was seated with them, smiling with satisfaction as he firmly clutched a handful of coins.

"My goodness, Master Hierophant, you have used my own earth magic to whisk me away from my castle's treasury." The King of Pentacles chuckled lightly as he turned to Follin in greeting. "Well met, young man, and welcome to my Kingdom."

Follin was unsure at first but slowly warmed to the King of Pentacles as they shared The Hierophant's pot of tea and small apple and cinnamon cakes in the garden of the hermitage.

"Your Majesty, I was asking Master Hierophant what your picture meant. It looks like you're hoarding your possessions but I'm not sure if this is control or greed or what?" asked Follin, feeling more confident with his query now that the picture had come alive.

The King nodded imperceptibly as he listened to Follin's question. "It is both, both wanting to hoard and to control your possessions. It can be interpreted either way. Both are common when one has possession of something precious. If it is knowledge then one must consider with whom to share it. Sometimes it is best to sit quietly and say nothing. At other times it is required that you share of what you know. If it be your precious possessions, once again, it is your choice if it is appropriate to share or not."

"Your Majesty, does that mean it is about valuing your knowledge and possessions then making wise choices as to how you use it or share it?"

"It certainly does, Follin, but remember that sometimes divination of a picture is best interpreted in consideration of other pictures sitting beside it. But now it is time for me to return to my treasury to count my blessings," said the King of Pentacles with a twinkle in his eyes as he disappeared.

Later that night as Follin recorded the lessons he had learnt that evening, he paused. "What else could be hoarded?" he mused. "The bullies hoarded the good opinion of Sir Dale to themselves, but they could have had my good opinion as well." Surprised, but pleased at his insights, he duly noted that in his journal, too.

FIVE OF PENTACLES

Hardship, support, rejection, fearing rejection and loss, failing to notice support when it is offered.

The Pentacles castle was on high alert when Sir Dale arrived with his wagon train. A band of Wildlanders had been seen roving in the nearby foothills of the Hindamar Mountains. Some of the farms had been raided and everyone was showing signs of stress.

As the wagons were unloaded, goods stacked and soldiers sent on errands, Follin and Eve were eventually escorted to their rooms by a rushed servant lad. The boy did not stay nor did he offer any help nor directions. The two guests felt cold, lonely and a little neglected. There was no food nor hot water for a bath, so they sat quietly around their lighted candle wondering what they should do. They began to feel unloved and even a burden to have been left alone like this.

With their usual efficiency, the Pentacles made their arrival, in the middle of a military crisis, a smooth transition from disorder into order. There was no panic, nor fear, that the Wildlanders would attack the castle itself, but, nevertheless, the captain of the castle guards made sure his men were fully prepared.

"Men, you know what to do, you've trained for this many a time, so get on with it. Sergeant Rollin, I know that it's late but see that your men attend early morning roll call and ensure that they have had a wash and a meal before retiring," ordered Captain Lohan in his clipped, sharp voice. He kept it just soft enough not to disturb the castle residents.

"Sir, we'll be in bed shortly. The stores are being put away as we speak; the horses fed and watered; wagons and equipment oiled and polished. I'll see that it's all done properly before I retire," replied the stoic Sergeant.

When Page Alice finally came to the lovers' room she saw them both sleeping on top of the bed. She lit the fire, gently woke her guests and laid out the food she had brought for their supper.

"Well, it's time for my bed, Eve. We've a big day ahead and you'll want to meet everyone and take a walk around the grounds. It's not big but it's nice here, welcome to my home." Alice gave Eve a peck on the cheek and left them to enjoy their cold meat, bread, cheese, and jug of brown ale.

"I was wondering if we would be fed tonight," yawned Follin as he put the kettle on the fire to boil. "I can't wait for the morning, this place looks fascinating, even in the dark. I bet it's ten times better in the light of day."

"Well, let's just finish supper first. There's a bowl of hot water over there by the windowsill for our hands and feet. We'd better have a wash and some food, then it's bedtime for us, I'm bushed," mumbled a very tired Eve.

―

The next morning they woke to the sounds of the household and a noisy rooster, crowing earnestly on the high wall outside. Follin rose and looked sleepily out of the window, telling the cock to be quiet. Surprised, he discovered their rooms opened onto a secluded, overgrown courtyard. He quickly woke Eve, jumping on the bed like an excited child seeing snow on a winter morn for the first time.

"Eve, darling! Look, a courtyard all to ourselves. Come on, there are chickens and a rooster. I wonder if they live here too." He pulled her upright and helped her put on a warm coat. Eve was not always at her best in the mornings, but seeing her husband so excited she caught his enthusiasm. Together they went out to explore their courtyard.

"Hey, look, under the vines, it's a table and some chairs. It looks just like Mage Hermes' workbench. When I visited him years ago he had a place just like this. And look, over there, the two pillars look like Hera's archway to her sacred glade. This place is magic, I can feel it!" He shuddered, not from the cold but from the energy that suddenly surged through him. Instead of feeling elated, however, it made him feel cold and clammy.

"Yes, I can feel it too, there's earth magic here, it's strong but…" Eve stopped talking to close her eyes, the better to feel the pervading energy field.

Follin sat on one of the chairs after clearing the vines from it.

"Eve, the magic… I don't know how to describe it, but it's not like what I felt in Hera's Sanctuary. There's something wrong with it."

"That's what the High Priestess told me. She said we had to help her heal the Empire's energy somehow. I can feel the castle's energy but… I think it's depressing." She slumped down in the chair next to Follin and her face fell into a look of forlorn helplessness.

"This is hopeless, I don't think I'll be of much use to anyone. I'm not a magician, I'm not even anything like you are. You're smart and clever, you've spent almost half of your life living this path of the mystic. Your father was a mage, you already have magic in your blood. But me, I'm just a grubby, herb-scrubber with dirt under her fingernails."

Follin looked at his wife as she bent forward, her face in her hands. He went over to her and gently stroked her hair.

"Eve, what is it?" he asked, lifting her chin so he could look into her eyes.

She saw the concern in his eyes and smiled awkwardly. "Can't you feel it? Are you blind to the hopelessness of this place? It's lost, Follin, it has lost its magic and now it's helpless."

Follin was struck with the force of her despair. Looking around he saw the magician's chair and sat down. He closed down his mind as he simultaneously raised his awareness. Follin could feel the magic. It was unwholesome, yes, but it was not hopeless. It just was not right. As he delved deeper he became nauseous and dizzy, but persevered, calming himself. Then he reached deep into the castle's complex network of magic. He felt for the castle's change point. It was elusive but he caught it and held it. Then as he shifted his own change point the castle's unwholesome energy returned to a state of balance.

With a flash of insight Follin came back to consciousness. He anchored the castle's energy balance in the two pillars that were part of the stonework of the courtyard and castle walls. He was not sure how long it would stay that way, but he now knew it could be tuned to a peaceful harmony as often as needed while they were staying there.

Follin looked across at Eve. "Is that better?"

Eve smiled wanly and nodded. "Yes, that's better."

While Eve went with Alice to explore the castle, Follin decided that he needed to talk with Mage Hermes and went to find him in his rooms.

"Follin, I'm sorry but I can't help you at the moment," answered the Emperor's Mage. He was busy trying to gather a pile of parchment scrolls in his arms, but they seemed to have a mind of their own. "I've got work of my own to do, and, as you know, Eve is very much part of it right now. There is so much preparation ahead of us. You have your own work to do, and I've got to get these blasted scrolls to Eve for her studies."

Mage Hermes looked at Follin over a small pair of glasses perched on the end of his nose as three more scrolls fell and rolled across the floor.

"Besides, I understand the Emperor wanted you to undertake an individual quest earning you right of entry into his magical assembly. He's grooming you for more than magic, my son," he said as Follin bent to the floor for the umpteenth time to gather the scrolls as even more dropped from the Mage's arms.

"I thought I was supposed to help you and Hera repair the Sanctuary and the Empire? I thought my magic was needed?" Follin replied, his face now creased in confusion.

"Your magic is indeed needed, Follin, but the Emperor needs you to develop it in a particular way. That's why he sent you on this journey to the four Kingdoms - and beyond. Now you had better find Sir Dale, he'll explain what your next task is. I think you might like it. And don't worry about Eve, I've given her a few tasks of her own to do. When the sun sets, my sister, Hera, is teaching her as well. That poor girl has so much to learn, yet so little time."

The old Mage's eyes twitched as together they carried the scrolls and equipment from his alchemy rooms to Follin and Eve's sunlit courtyard.

"Eve is very sensitive to all forms of energy," he explained, "and we need her to study its subtle forms as it ebbs and flows in each Kingdom, beginning with this one, the Pentacles."

The Mage eased himself into the chair and arranged the scrolls across the table surface. As he did so his sharp eyes lifted to stare at Follin.

"My son, is this your work? I can feel the changes you've made here in the courtyard. Hmm, very interesting indeed..." the Mage closed his eyes all the better to feel the weaving of energy that Follin had performed that morning.

"I can feel the subtle fabric of the Pentacles energy. You've managed to anchor it here. Now that, my son, was very clever. In fact, I don't think I need to do any work on it myself, it's perfectly suited to my lessons."

The cock perched on the high stone wall crowed in agreement as his hens scratched busily in the courtyard's unkempt garden beds. The morning sun rose over the courtyard wall and illuminated the two stone pillars. It was a beautiful day in the Pentacles Kingdom.

"Son, the Pentacles Kingdom has much to teach you and Eve. I think you will both enjoy your time here. Now it's time for you to find Eve and bring her here for her lessons. Then you had better find Sir Dale to begin your own."

Sir Dale was with his two squires, Mavor and Allen. They scowled silently when they saw Follin walk into the weapons room with Sergeant Rollin.

"Follin, I was just about to send Allen to fetch you." Sir Dale turned to his squires. "Lads, I am very proud of your performance the other day on our journey home. Allen, you and Mavor excelled in swordsmanship in holding the enemy's advance on the track while our troops moved forward to chase the rest back into the forest. You exhibited the kind of courage and bravery we are so proud of in our Pentacles soldiers."

Sir Dale then turned to his new attendant who appeared to shudder slightly under his gaze. Follin did not want to be singled out, it made him vulnerable, open to criticism and humiliation by these two ruffians.

"Your engagement with the enemy was somewhat unusual. We were informed that you had magic, but what you did the other day protected my troops and I am always glad when bloodshed is prevented."

Mavor's eyes narrowed as he watched Sir Dale heap praise on what he believed was just a 'spoiled, jumped-up islander yokel'.

"Follin, I am sending you with Sergeant Rollin, he will introduce you to our bladesmith, Master Pew. He will teach you some of the magic of our

Kingdom: the magic of turning the earth into tools for our gardens to grow our food, and into weapons for our security." Sir Dale turned back to his two squires and continued with his instructions.

Sergeant Rollin saluted, then motioned Follin to walk with him towards the nearby sound of a hammer striking iron.

"So, lad, you've not done any sword training or bladesmithing in your village before you came to the Empire?" asked Rollin politely. Even he was a little apprehensive around the young man since hearing about how cleverly Follin had used earth magic on their way through the forest.

"Nay, Sergeant Rollin, I've swung an axe but never a blacksmith's hammer. I did a little sword practice with Ivan, the Emperor's swordsmaster, but that's all. Ivan said I needed to practise a lot more if I was to be of any use as a man-at-arms. I must admit that I find wielding a sword is really difficult." Here, Follin paused to gather his thoughts before he continued speaking. He liked Rollin. The older man was powerfully built and a wonderful swordsman with a manner that made Follin feel accepted.

"I am a bit frightened though, I've not encountered alchemy like the making of steel before. I hope I don't make a fool of myself," said Follin, recalling how he had failed so miserably at wood and metal-craft at school. He could not hit a nail on the head let alone heat a blade in a firepit.

"Now, lad," Sergeant Rollin said soothingly when he noticed Follin's unease. "Just you follow Master Pew's lessons. He's a fine old man with a gift indeed. If there's anyone who can teach you smithing, it's ol' Pew." Rollin had overheard the Emperor telling Sir Dale that he believed Follin found learning magic as easy as falling off a horse - and he had seen him fall off a horse, more than once, on their journey to the Pentacles Kingdom.

They walked towards a covered pavilion with a furnace, firepit, hammers and anvils. The noise of the apprentice pumping the bellows and the cloud of smoke and steam enveloping everything signaled that the bladesmith was hard at work. To Follin the smoke-blackened walls and ceiling indicated that the smithy had been in use for many generations.

"Aye, 'tis the lad from the Isle. Welcome my boy, though boy you aren't I can see and from what I've 'eard. You know some magic already I believe?" Old Master Pew held a heavy hammer in his right hand letting its head rest on the enormous anvil at his side. Without waiting for Follin to answer, Pew nodded for Rollin to head back to his soldiering and continued to chat with this new apprentice.

"You don't need to know much magic just yet, young lad. I'll teach thee what thou don't know and tha'll pick up the rest, no doubt. Sir Dale said you're a bright one so let's get started." With barely a pause he pointed to a solid-looking stool for Follin to sit on. "Now just sit there and watch what me and the apprentice 'ere be doing till I tell thee to move. And don't touch metal till thee has learned to recognise if it's hot or cold."

Follin spent most of each day observing, fetching charcoal, shoveling it into the furnace, tidying the smithy and sweeping the floor. He was general rouseabout for both the smiling apprentice, Justin, and the bladesmith himself, Master Pew. Although initially disappointed that he would not be learning to handle the steel from day one, Follin set to with a will, doing his tasks diligently. As each day passed he joined in with the light-hearted banter and humour of the old master and the young apprentice.

In his second week, Follin asked the bladesmith a question that had been on his mind since he had arrived at the smithy.

"Master Pew, what is a bladesmith? Is it any different from a blacksmith?"

Old Pew looked across the red flames of the firepit, put his hammer and tongs down beside his anvil and sat down on an aged wooden stool.

He pulled a face as he nodded to the two boys to sit and listen. It was early morn and the firepit was still warming up.

Pointing his chin to Justin, his apprentice, Old Pew said, "Now my lad 'ere knows not to ask a master a question like that. Not 'ere in the Pentacles Kingdom where children are taught in their first year to recognise tree and timber; gem and jewel; leather and cloth; timber and metal masters of every form and manner - by name and by nature." He winked at Justin.

"A blacksmith can turn raw minerals into metals and can forge iron into anything he wishes. Some blacksmiths are happiest at repairing damaged tools, ploughshares, shears, frying pans and kettles or makin' practical things like gates or fire irons. Others like to do decorative work. But a bladesmith is a weapons specialist, a master of steel, the killing sword, spear and arrowheads." Master Pew paused, as if expecting a question from Follin, then continued.

"I know I've not spoken of the differences between metals that we've worked; nor 'ave I explained the temperatures for each tool or weapon blade; the number of forge pumps per minute needed for each task; nor the reason you've been throwing in different powders and shoveling loads of charcoal - but today is as good a day as any to begin."

Over the following months, Follin learned of the specific metal ores, minerals and other ingredients that went into repairing shovel blades and why a different set of ingredients were required to repair and create armour, spearheads and sword blades. Follin learned how to pump the bellows using different rhythms, when to add more charcoal and when to leave well enough alone. His tasks were many, but he loved going to the forge every day. Slowly the castle folk became accustomed to his whistling on his way to work each morning.

Follin's meditation – Five of Pentacles

The image showed two poor souls walking past what appeared to be a hospice, a place where people in need sought shelter and healing. They appeared to be suffering in the snow from wounds and poverty.

Placing the image firmly in his mind's eye he slowly eased into a deep trance. Once again he was at the hermitage cottage of his previous journey through the Major Arcana. This time he was alone.

He placed the image in front of him and studied it from all angles.

'I can't see much good in this picture. It sure looks like hardship and poverty of possessions as well as their spirit,' he muttered to himself. 'They may even be refugees displaced by war or retired soldiers unemployed and down on their luck.'

As he considered the image he had a flash of insight: 'hardship, indeed, but right beside them is an opportunity to ease that hardship… that hospice is also a place where they could receive assistance is it not? And there, look, one seeks to help the other.' He watched as the person in front waited for the one legged man to catch up as they trudged through the snow.

'Perhaps it means that through hardship there is always opportunity, and that genuine friendship enables opportunity.'

Feeling quite content with himself, Follin went for a walk through his hermitage forest in the astral plane, for the sheer pleasure of it.

SIX OF PENTACLES

Resources, generosity, power, giving responsibly.

While Follin was busy learning the mastery of metal, Eve was busy studying with Mage Hermes and High Priestess Hera. Mage Hermes was forever delivering more of his precious scrolls to complement his tutoring. They usually spent their day studying in Follin and Eve's wild but cosy sunlit courtyard. It was also the favoured hunting ground for the rooster and his hens who had greeted them on their first morning. When Eve got bored with her lessons she enjoyed watching the hens scratching and pecking in the overgrown garden beds.

"My dear Eve, can you please get that scroll I've managed to drop outside the door? That's it, thank you, dear girl. I'd hate to see the hens making nests out of my precious papers. If you're not careful an entire collection of wisdom will make its way into a hen box, one never knows what wise chick might hatch from one of those nests. That reminds me, when I was just a boy I was apprenticed to Mage Willowtree. He now lives in a cave up in the mountains close by... I think... or was he the one who turned himself into a willow tree... oh dear, I just can't remember."

The aged Mage often reminisced in the company of his young apprentices. Both Follin and Eve made Mage Hermes feel comfortable, alive, and useful. His journeys across the dimensions to find the magic that would counter the poison in the Empire, had sorely affected him. He now knew beyond doubt that his current incarnation was soon to come to an end. He was not afraid; in fact, he was excited. As a magician of high degree, Mage Hermes had crossed the border separating life and death many times. He had wandered amid the beauty of the Elysian Fields and through the hellfire of Tartarus itself. He was no longer afraid of the Borderlands, the place between the worlds. Although he had two potential Mages here, what did worry him was that he might not complete his task of training his replacement.

This was a rarity, only once before in the history of all the lands had a man and his wife carried the sacred burden of managing the magical responsibilities for the Empire - and beyond. The Magician was not the property of any one kingdom, or Empire, their responsibility was to humanity and the land they held in trust. Hera, his sister in magic, was his shadow, his mirror on the other side. When he passed from the world, so, too, would she.

Theirs was the sacred task to train these two promising souls to replace them when their season of life was ended. But would they take up the task presented to them? Would they agree to end their relationship with this earthly existence to become one with the many other dimensions beyond consciousness?

Unaware of The Magician's ruminations, Eve smiled as she helped Hermes set up his scrolls, maps and documents on the bench as he continued to reminisce.

"At least I think Mage Willowtree lives in a cave in the mountains hereabouts. Or was that Mage Wormwood? Oh my goodness, I do believe it is Mage Wormwood. I wonder whatever happened to my old master, Willowtree?"

"You told me yesterday that Mage Willowtree had assumed his transition from this life to the next by entering a willow tree, remember? You said that you still talk with him in your dreams." Eve often tried to keep Mage Hermes on task, although it seemed almost impossible at times.

"Oh yes, that's right, he crossed the borders of consciousness way before you were even born, my dear girl. But I do recall I spoke with him, yes, of course, it was on one of my journeys in the Borderlands. He said he was worried about your progress in learning the old earth magic. I reassured him that your magical studies are progressing smoothly. Old Willowtree does get excited at times but he'll now settle back into his willow tree. There he'll soak up the water from the soil, the sunshine from the skies and meditate some more before he contacts me again. I told him of what you and Follin felt here on your first morning. He said he needed to contemplate that before calling for me again."

Mage Hermes carefully laid out his scrolls in their order and began the lessons for the day. Eve's was a path of theory followed by practice. Hermes well understood that her knowledge of practical healing was strong. She knew the herbs of the forest, the ways of their growth, the times to sow and harvest and their healing properties. What impressed him more than anything was Eve's exceptional intuitive skill. She could determine the different healing properties of a herb grown in different locations or harvested at different phases of the moon. Only adepts knew a certain plant could heal one ailment when grown in shade but could worsen the condition when grown in full sunlight.

Mage Hermes had also tested her on several occasions by leaving various concoctions on her table, waiting quietly as she felt and intuited their properties. There were even times when she corrected him on certain aspects of a herbal preparation. On his return to his rooms he would ponder over his scrolls and manuscripts to find that she was always right. While Eve could intuit much of her knowledge she still needed to learn the basics - just as he had been taught.

―――

Eve's lessons did not stop when she finished with Mage Hermes in the afternoon. Hera, the High Priestess, was her teacher in the quiet moments between consciousness and the unconscious in the evenings.

"My dearest girl," Mage Hermes said soon after their introductions, "my task is to put the information into your head for practical applications on the conscious earth plane. My sister, Hera, will teach you how to use it in the spirit worlds beyond consciousness." He had not really said much more about the difference between their roles. In fact, Eve considered it odd that even though Mage Hermes and Hera were spoken of as brother and sister, she just could not quite reconcile them as siblings.

―――

Since her conversation with Frailbones on their journey to the castle, Eve had opened up and was beginning to trust and bond with the Pentacles women of the castle. Over lunch one day Eve asked Page Alice what she knew of the two 'magical ones' – Mage Hermes and Hera - as many of the Pentacles court called them in hushed tones. She specifically wanted to know if they really were brother and sister.

"Eve, you know more than me, I really don't know much about them at all, I'm sorry. You could ask The Hierophant when he next visits, but we don't know when that will be. And given it's been so dangerous lately we don't really expect him to be visiting soon," was all Alice could offer.

"You could have asked me," announced the Queen of Pentacles who was sitting a few seats farther up the table. "I've been listening to you all through my meal and not once have you even thought to ask me a question."

Eve's face flushed bright red, she could feel the heat rising. She was so embarrassed at her error that it almost felt like steam was lifting off the top of her head.

"I am so sorry, Your Majesty, it never occurred to me to ask you. I always thought you would be way too busy to even consider a silly question from the likes of me. I'm not royalty nor am I high born. My family are from forest and village, none of them have ever been royalty," she stammered.

The Queen visibly balked, she shuffled her feet awkwardly beneath the table, then caught herself. "My dear, that is completely understandable. I myself am not of high birth either."

She looked kindly at Eve and smiled, a warm smile. "I thought you were ignoring me, young lady. I did feel a little left out of the conversation, but now I do understand. Please, in future, you must come and sit opposite me, I think we may have a lot more in common than you think."

Alice smiled behind her hand as she noticed several of the court ladies choke on their poached trout crepes and leek soup. Lady Holland, head of the royal household, spoke firmly to bring order to the dining table.

"Your Majesty, ladies of the court, may I take this opportunity to remind us all of proper dining protocol. Our Kingdom is finely balanced between reckless abandon and cautious stability through thoroughly thought out rules and protocols. These bring order and structure to a very chaotic world. Any tampering with table seating can quickly upset the order our kitchen staff have so carefully prepared for our dining harmony and compatibility." Being careful not to look at the Queen, Lady Holland continued. "Why, promoting young Eve to the position opposite the heads of this Kingdom, as proposed, will mean Lady Mandorene will need to move one place to the left. And that will mean Lady Renault will be displaced to the corner seat." She now looked at the Queen and her voice took on a teacher's tone, explaining that the change could easily end in chaos.

"The entire table arrangement will need to be, well, rearranged. My kitchen and dining staff have already gone to considerable lengths to fit young Eve in at the table as it is, but to move her to a seat facing Your Majesty, why, that is simply…" she stopped speaking when she saw the Queen purse her lips and glare at her.

"My dear, Lady Holland, you have been the absolute cornerstone of my family and the royal court for many years. Your outstanding achievements have brought stability and structure in delivering our daily nourishment and entertainment. I really don't know how I could have managed to survive without you."

It was Lady Holland's turn to blush, her face breaking into an enormous smile. Her eyes began to flutter as she felt she might swoon bathed in the glow of her Queen's praise.

"I know you will be able to come up with a suitable and just plan for our table arrangements by tomorrow. But for today we'll pretend that we can change protocols and we shall take supper with our families in the garden." The Queen noticed some of the girls, handmaidens and ladies, brighten at the thought of doing something different. "Although we Pentacles aren't known for our flexibility, once we make up our minds we can do anything. What do you think, Lady Holland, do you think your staff could manage a light supper by candle and firelight this evening?"

Once again Lady Holland blushed. "Oh, Your Majesty, it is my absolute honour to prepare whatever it is you wish. I'll see to its management immediately."

As she stood, Lady Renault spoke, "Your Majesty, if I may suggest a fireside singalong? Guitars, trumpets and drums? I daresay, that would be so much fun."

That triggered excited chatter among the staff and the men and ladies at the royal dinner table.

"And why not! Let's do it, thank you. Ladies and gentlemen, we shall collect our partners and gather around the campfires in the floral garden for supper and a singalong this evening," announced the Queen.

Turning to Eve she asked, "Do you sing?"

"Your Majesty, indeed I do, but I don't know any court songs. I've but songs of the forests and the fields. If that be your pleasure then I shall be honoured to sing for you," replied Eve, smiling at both the Queen and Alice, who was barely able to sit still with excitement.

With their meal over, Alice escorted Eve to her rooms. She was so excited she could not stop herself.

"Eve, do you know, this has never happened before, not in my lifetime it hasn't. No one has ever been asked to change seats at the table and we rarely go outside to have supper in the gardens. And, what's even more amazing, Lady Renault has never suggested we do anything different, she's a first class stick-in-the-mud. Just think of it, a singalong and a campfire!" Alice held Eve's hand and squeezed. "It's as if a depression has been lifted from weighing down on our shoulders. Your coming here has been such a grand thing!"

That evening it seemed like the entire kingdom was at the gardens in the castle keep. To accommodate so many guests, the court staff had many campfires with ample seating for almost the entire kingdom it seemed.

A troupe of singers and musicians wandered from fire to fire, wine was served and beer swilled. It was the rule of the Kingdom that when a singing troupe stopped at a table the people there had to sing for their supper. The entertainment was diverse, rude, raucous and often the group would deliver lines from a famous speech, play, poem or sing a famous Pentacles ballad. Sometimes all present would gather around the performers and join in.

It was said to be one of the best evenings of entertainment the Kingdom had ever had. Both the King and Queen of Pentacles participated in all events and provided awards for those who sang or played their instruments particularly well.

Just as the sun broke above the edge of the world to announce a new day the revelers began to head off to bed. Arm in arm Follin and Eve walked to their room. On their way they saw Captain Bleecher bellowing his orders for the day. They had heard of these impromptu changing of the guard displays and were keen not to miss it. They stopped with other late revelers to watch the performance.

"Sergeant of the Guard!" roared Captain Bleecher. Sergeant Rollin walked over, his knees stiff with arthritis, and saluted his captain.

"Sergeant, have you sent a section of men-at-arms to run the perimeter to ensure nothing untoward has occurred while our people were busy entertaining?"

"Sir, it's done, sir. I've sent out two sections throughout the night and all is well, sir." The aged sergeant remained stifly at attention.

Captain Bleecher nodded, he already knew this but he liked to give his senior noncommissioned officers the opportunity to announce their achievements to the castle audience.

"Nice work, Sergeant. You and your men may retire to bed, and a well-earned rest it is. Please send me Sergeant Lards, I believe he is Duty Sergeant for today?"

"Yes, sir, he is. He's on his way now, sir, just coming up beside you. And thank you, sir, we shall now take that well-earned rest." Sergeant Rollin saluted once more, dismissed his patrol, then limped to his home where he knew his wife would have a hot bath, oils and herbs for his aching bones.

The Duty Sergeant saluted stiffly, his platoon aligned smartly behind him.

"Captain Bleecher! Sergeant Lards and morning watch, ready as ordered, Sir!" Sergeant Lards snapped another salute that was just as smarty returned.

"Sir," Sergeant Lards continued, "we respectfully request a parade inspection, sir. It has been a full week since our last inspection and we're smartin' and sweatin' for a proper parade. Thank you, sir."

"Of course, Sergeant Lards." Captain Bleecher knew that Sergeant Lards loved parades. His platoon, no matter from which section of the kingdom they came from, was always the best dressed, marched the smartest and were drilled to perfection.

Turning to the platoon the sergeant bellowed, "Platoon... attention!"

Thirty pairs of feet snapped to attention, drawing a light ripple of 'oohs' and 'ahs' of admiration from the gathered crowd.

"Platoon... stand at... ease!"

Again, the sound of thirty pairs of feet cracked loudly in the chill morning air as the soldiers stood smartly on parade. Hands swept into place; spears held tightly in one hand, the other hand pointing straight down their trouser seams.

"Platoon, ranks of three.. and step lively now, you're on parade… Platoon! Order, three ranks for the captain's inspection… march!"

The platoon sharply rearranged themselves from two ranks into three with a precision that Follin and Eve found impossible to follow.

The crowd cheered with a joy that was infectious. Follin and Eve found they too could not help but cheer along with their friends. This did not go unnoticed by Sergeant Lards or Captain Bleecher, nor even the troops themselves. Several of the young soldiers fought back smiles of pride.

Sergeant Lards now swung smartly to his captain and together they inspected their platoon.

"Dust particle on that boot, Private," announced Captain Bleecher, as he walked slowly past the first line of soldiers.

"Wipe yon foot on yon trouser leg and thou'll get two weeks latrine duty, Private Hoggs!" bellowed Sergeant Lards. The poor private quickly dropped his heel back down and almost lost the grip of his spear.

"Is that a whisker I see on your chin private? I do believe it is…" Captain Bleecher loved these little displays, and so did his troops. "Ah, my mistake. Private Twomby, isn't it? Hero of Haddens Gap last year? Held off seven Wildlanders while our boys built a defensive perimeter for the wagons? Nice work that was too, Private. No, it seems that is a bit of fluff blown in by the wind."

Private Twomby puffed up his chest with pride; any larger and his chest would have burst.

"And what is this?" bellowed the captain. "Is that a razor cut? Did you cut yourself shaving in the dark, Corporal Anders?"

"I'm very sorry, Captain Bleechers, that be a wound from an arrow from yesterday's skirmish in the hills. I'm terribly sorry but I've not quite healed yet, sir," replied the nervous corporal.

The captain knew Corporal Anders carried wounds. His arm was still stiff from an earlier skirmish with the Wildlanders and this was an opportunity to praise him. Captain Bleecher's preferred method of ensuring respect for the Kingdom's soldiers was to praise them at these impromptu inspections in front of their appreciative community.

"Sir, if I may explain," bellowed Sergeant Lards, who was also a knowing participant in this game. "Corporal Anders and three troops were sent to escort one of our wounded back to the wagons. On their way they were ambushed by a group of Wildlanders. The corporal sent his troops to carry the wounded fellow back to the safety of the wagons while he held the Wildlanders off with his sword. Sir, he withstood many a spirited charge by the enemy while managing to injure several of them for their discourtesy. An arrow grazed his chin, as can be seen, but he is Pentacles born and bred and he'll heal soon enough. His leadership and performance was an outstanding example of heroism. Corporal Anders did not retire until he had seen the Wildlander's backs when they returned in haste to the forest."

"Hmm, seems you have here a platoon of outstanding Pentacles soldiers, Sergeant Lards," announced Captain Bleecher loudly. He was pleased to hear the applause and cheering from what was now almost a hundred spectators.

"Yes, sir, an outstanding platoon but only one among an outstanding army of heroes, if I may suggest, sir," said Sergeant Lards just as loudly, again to cheering and even louder applause.

The display over, the platoon was sent to their posts, their chests aching and their walk strong and proud.

"Captain Bleecher," called Follin as he led Eve across the makeshift parade ground towards him. "Sir, thank you, that was a most remarkable parade we just witnessed. Is this a Pentacles thing? You know, being so supportive and nice to each other?" asked Follin with a look of amazement in his eyes.

"Son, we are at war, it is a nasty war too. Many of us in the Kingdoms are of mixed blood and that creates tension. We can't tell who are the Wildlander fighters and who are the peaceful Wildlander villagers. We understand that the Wildanders are simply trying to survive just like we are." Noticing the fatigue in their faces he started to walk the two newcomers to their rooms.

"Over the past twelve months we have lost more than fifty soldiers in ambushes. What is worse, we've lost dozens of families that once were free to work their farms outside the city walls. You see, the Wildlanders are being pushed by other clans and peoples moving onto their land. The only direction they can escape is through us. Either they conquer our Kingdom and make it their own, or they perish. I've studied their ways and they aren't all bad, but they certainly aren't going to walk through our lands thinking it their right to take what they want."

"But why don't they just talk to you and make some sort of peace?" asked Eve.

"Good question, lass. We've tried, the best Swords negotiators and even the Emperor himself has tried. For years we've seen this coming and not once have the Wildlanders tried to meet us half way in our peace talks. Instead, the more pressure they're under from the Outsiders north of them, the more ferocious they are against us. It's not just the Pentacles, it's all four Kingdoms, the Wands, Cups and Swords - we're all under pressure. We've had quite a few years of fighting, vicious fighting, against the various Wildlander tribes, and sometimes we've fought Outlander tribes way beyond our borders… but don't get me wrong, they're right tough sods. They fight and they kill and they want our lands and our castles. Their magic is somewhat different from ours, and their mages are proper evil swine, believe me."

The captain stopped and nodded to the two Mystic Islanders as they reached their rooms. "We need your magic to counter theirs, and to do that we need you to understand and embrace the Tarot Empire's magic.

That's why we've agreed to open our hearts and our homes to you. You are Mystic Islanders, which to us Pentacles means that you have a wild magic. Everything about you is shrouded in mystery."

"Captain Bleecher," Follin felt a little awkward about where the conversation was heading and wished to change the subject. "I can see some of the Emperor in you. I saw it this morning in how you addressed your men. I admire that and I wanted to say 'thank you'."

Eve was not as squeamish as her husband and drew the captain back to the topic. "Follin and I have both witnessed the bad side of these Wildlanders. I lost my family to them and Follin lost his brother, and his father left because of them." Eve paused, she then yawned as she suddenly realised how late it was. "I'm sorry, Captain, we'd better get to bed, we have our lessons in a few hours. Mage Hermes and Old Pew are both as savage with latecomers as any Wildlander."

The captain left them at their door and bid them to 'sleep well'. With a gladdened heart he went back to his soldiering.

Follin's meditation – Six of Pentacles

Follin sat with the picture of a merchant holding a set of scales in one hand and with the other he handed out coins. There were two other people in this image. One was dressed in rags and had what appeared to be a bandage around his head. Perhaps he was a soldier returned from service protecting the Kingdom? The other was also in rags. Both rejoiced at receiving their gift, or was it payment?

Setting the image in his mind's eye he found himself inside the picture. Follin stood quietly to one side listening to the conversation between the man and those to whom he was giving the coins.

"Your efforts are well noted and rewarded. Accept these few coins as a token of our Kingdom's respect and gratitude. I know that you will use them wisely," he heard the man say.

'So this might mean payment? Perhaps giving coins as a reward for doing good deeds or doing a good service for someone?' Follin thought. When he saw the merchant about to walk off Follin called out and walked over to join him.

"Kind sir, I saw you handing money over to these people. I was wondering if you would tell me what your act might mean?" he asked politely.

The man studied Follin carefully as though he were about to place the youth on the scales he held in his hand.

"Young man, the meaning of my act was to demonstrate that one needs to understand what it means to 'give'. Gifting is not necessarily of money, it is done in many guises: a handshake, a welcome, a kind word perhaps, just as Captain Bleecher rewards his men."

The man considered what to say next, then continued. "A person gives for many reasons. Some give to alleviate their own burden of guilt but that is not my way. My gifting style seeks to maximise positive outcomes that will benefit my community in the long term. We have little control of what people do with our gifts, however, a gift given in the right manner and for the right reason, to the right person at the right moment on their journey through life, has the greatest potential to be used as it is intended - honourably and respectfully."

The man tipped his hat in farewell, but before the image faded he turned to say one more thing. In place of the merchant stood the smiling figure of the King of Pentacles.

"Follin, the act of giving comes with an enormous responsibility both to the receiver and to the giver. For some, to receive a gift of value is a responsibility too great for their strength of will – it becomes an unwanted burden thrust upon them. In some situations it is the withholding of the gift that is the most responsible course of action."

The King of Pentacles held up his scales for Follin to see. "See these scales? Have you pondered the meaning of why I hold them in one hand as I give with the other? It is because they can measure the value of the gift to the giver, not just the person receiving it."

As the images faded, Follin reached for his journal. He thought back to his time at school, to the children whose parents had given them coins to spend as they wished. Some had sensibly saved them. Others had bought sweet treats and shared them with their friends. Some had given them to poor people and some had used their coins to buy wine or ale for themselves.

His thoughts turned to those he knew who had received charity. Some had repaid their benefactors in coin or labour, others had passed on the gift of charity to others when they could. Next he thought of some families in his village who had become submissive, lazy and reliant on the generosity of others.

He recalled how his poor neighbours had given to those in need and of wealthy neighbours who had given nothing. He thought of those who gave selfless for a greater good, and of those who accumulated wealth purely for selfish gain.

Follin dutifully recorded his thoughts, yawned and fell asleep.

SEVEN OF PENTACLES

Evaluation, preparation, possibilities, validation, where to next.

Follin was disappointed that Master Pew had not let him do much more than clean the smithy and feed the forge. The most exciting thing he had done thus far was to work at the bellows, pumping air for Pew and Justin to heat the iron for bladesmithing. Days had led into weeks and weeks into months, but all the same, he picked up the manner of smithing by that age-old teaching tool – observation. He learnt how to pump for hours at the bellows without tiring; to fire up the forge and bring it to temperature using the correct tinder, charcoal and air. Then he learnt to hammer the white-hot iron into ingots ready for Pew and Justin to make into tools and weapons. Follin worked with a will as his chest broadened and his arms thickened. He now found that he could swing his hammer all day without tiring.

"Eve, I need a hot bath," Follin called as he began to undress after a particularly hard day, "and your healing hands on my back."

He threw his trousers across the bedroom floor, but Eve was nowhere to be seen. Then he heard a splash from the bathroom. His voice drifted off when he saw her waiting for him in the bath-tub. Built for one but large enough for two, he climbed gingerly into the bath-tub to join her. The young lovers giggled and splashed about like lovebirds courting in a birdbath. Despite their heavy workload there was always enough energy for lovemaking.

Eve had her trials too. Her work with Mage Hermes involved hours studying the history of earth magic, particularly the Pentacles style of earth magic. She met with the Kingdom's high officials, frequently with the King and Queen of Pentacles, attending most of their weekly ceremonies. Many times she asked Mage Hermes if he could get her out of their endless, boring committee meetings.

"My dear girl, I know what you mean. We of the Emperor's court call it, 'death by committee'. It's worse than the Wildlander's 'death by a thousand cuts' I'm told." Mage Hermes chuckled to himself. "You are gaining or rather absorbing the energy of the Pentacles Kingdom through your interactions with these people, though. Each office has certain magical qualities, no single official or craftsman or woman, has them all, none. Even the King and Queen need their officials around them to create balance and harmony in the Kingdom. Haven't you noticed that your lessons have come along by leaps and bounds after each ceremony? And yet there are things you know that you haven't even studied yet. That is the power of magic, to do without thinking, learning unconsciously. That's what my sister, Hera, is also doing in your dreams, teaching without your being aware of it."

The Mage studied his young apprentice. "Besides," he said, "the King and Queen of Pentacles are teaching you their particular earth magic too. You haven't noticed because you're caught up in the mundane goings on at the table and their ceremonies. But beneath, in the silent spaces within the conversations, you can find them conversing with you directly. That, my dear, is a lesson you can bring yourself to catch all by yourself. The next time you are in the royal presence stop your internal self-talk and go beneath the conversations around you. Go within and listen."

Eve turned her head to the side, all the better to think about what he had said. "Mage Hermes, I'll certainly try that listening thing, I've heard you speak of it before." She paused, "I wanted to ask you something, too. I've dreamed every night since I came here but still I'm not really sure about High Priestess Hera. She's beautiful but she is a shadow in a shadowy world. She's darkness and she is night. That is another one of her names, isn't it, Nyx, the Goddess of the Night?" Hermes nodded and waited for her to continue. "Well, it's just strange that my other teacher teaches me in my dreams. How can I learn when I'm sleeping? I don't understand."

The old man brushed some leaves and chicken mess off his chair in the lovers' courtyard, then invited Eve to sit next to him.

"My dear, Hera is not only of this world…" he put his finger to his chin before proceeding. "She is of this world but she doesn't need her body to do her work as High Priestess." When he noticed Eve turn a shade of white and her eyes glazing over, he hurried along. "No, she isn't dead. Hera has evolved along a different path from us. It's to do with the power of her Sanctuary. She studied magic through means even I don't understand. I've spoken to The Hierophant, he's lived the longest of the arcana folk and studied humanity more than I have. He said that he doesn't know how Hera did it but I have a feeling he knows more than he lets on. He speaks to the trees and the rocks, you know, oh yes, The Hierophant lived before man built cities - before humanity tilled the soil to plant the first harvest. That old man is as old as time itself and has accumulated more knowledge than anyone I know."

Eve's face brightened. "Follin met The Hierophant. He said he felt really comfortable with him. I'd like to meet him one day, too. Can we do that? Go and meet him?"

"Why do you want to visit that boring old man? He's not your teacher, my dear. You need to focus on what we're doing now." He tapped the table to make a point. "Don't forget, my dear girl, you have many teachers in the Empire. Myself and the High Priestess are your two pillars, your foundations. What we teach you is what the others will build upon. So, please, be patient."

Just then a blackbird alighted noisily on the courtyard wall. It spied the birdbath and dived down to perch on its edge. The little bird carefully checked its surroundings for danger. Eve saw it look at her with its piercing eyes and it seemed to wink at her. She felt her face frown as she tried to tell herself that it was not so.

"See, now you've mentioned The Hierophant, he's come to visit and check up on us," grunted the Mage. "Oh, all right, I'll leave you two to chat for a while. I'll meet you for lunch in the court gardens." With that Mage Hermes stood, arched backwards and Eve heard his bones crack loudly. She gritted her teeth, the sound made her feel like her own back was breaking.

"Certainly, Mage Hermes, but... it's only a blackbird..." She spoke to thin air, the mage had gone and now in his place stood The Hierophant. He was tall, taller than she expected. He wore a woodsman's apparel and boots of leather that looked strangely soft to the touch and extremely comfortable. He calmly stepped over to sit in the Mage's chair.

"And so we meet, Eve. I heard you talking of me and since I wanted to meet you, I decided now was as good a time as ever." He winked and looked across to the birdbath. She followed his look and saw the blackbird bathing, splashing water under its wings in delight.

"A little bird told me that you wanted to know something." He smiled at her look of surprise.

"Hello, Master Hierophant, Follin said you could cook a meal with just your imagination. He said that he saw you light a fire without a spark and handle a pot of boiling water without a rag to protect your skin."

"Aye, little tricks for a tired and despondent young man on a journey of discovery in the miserable rain and mist. That evening was enough to make anyone feel miserable. Follin reminded me of myself when I was young, carefree and not a thought for his next meal. Now let me hear your question, Eve, and just so that you know, I don't tell Mage Hermes everything – I like to keep some of my secrets, secret." The Hierophant's smile broadened and he made a conspiratorial wink again.

"Oh, I thought Mage Hermes knew everything," she replied innocently. The Hierophant certainly did not look 'as old as time itself', not the way Mage Hermes described him. In fact, he looked about middle-aged and not even as careworn as many hard-working men she knew.

"Well, in some ways, Mage Hermes does know everything, he is the Empire's Magician you know. But some of us archetypes have our ways and know things even magicians aren't to know. For instance, what does it feel like to swim under the water…" he paused for emphasis, "but to also breathe the very water you would drown in?"

Eve did not have an answer so he continued.

"Or the feel of sunshine on your skin - so strong that it penetrates into the marrow within your bones? Then to suck that sunshine up through your marrow into your spine and to send that light into every part of your body? Or, better still, what is it like to turn your fat into strength or your muscles into springs?" He stood and sprang into the air startling the blackbird to flight.

To Eve's eyes The Hierophant appeared to leap from tree top to tree top then return to his seat at the table.

Eve gasped. "What did you just do? Did you really jump into those trees and…" she stopped, bewildered, not trusting herself to even speak.

"Mage Hermes didn't tell you about that did he? No, but don't be fooled by that old man. To you he looks old, to Follin he appears middle-aged, to others, he will appear just as he wants them to see him. Or perhaps, how they want him to look. Magic is one part art and pageantry and many parts dedicated hard work.

"Now to your question, who is High Priestess Hera? Why does she teach you in your dreams and meditations?" The Hierophant looked at Eve with his piercing eyes.

"Yes, that is my question. Mage Hermes said she is his sister, yet they are so different," Eve replied.

"Yes, they were once brother and sister, both very talented. They came from the Isle of Runda, the island of secrets. The Magician and High Priestess at that time had almost completed their season in this plane of existence and were looking for a couple to replace them. They found that couple, and what was most interesting was that they were of the same blood. Hera and Hermes were brought from the island to the Empire of the Tarot many centuries ago. They were taught the magic of the four Kingdoms, much like you and Follin are doing right now. Sadly, the burden of magic causes a slow decline in the health of those who take on the responsibility of keeping the Tarot Empire safe. Hera and Hermes stepped up to replace the retiring Magician and High Priestess when they were required to do so."

The Hierophant had spoken softly but he had also engaged Eve in her dream mind. In her mind's eye she saw the two siblings as children doing magic tricks for their family and village friends. Then she saw them as teenagers, rebelling against their elders who gladly handed them over to The Magician and High Priestess as their end-years approached.

"So Mage Hermes was right, Hera is his sister," said Eve softly.

The Hierophant nodded then stood and walked inside, bringing back a pot of tea.

"Eve, I too have my lessons for you. A gift awaits, do you wish for it?"

When Eve nodded The Hierophant continued. "Please, put your hand out and feel this teapot, it's just warm isn't it?" He put it down on the table between them, Eve carefully touched its surface. It was barely warm, having been made by herself for Mage Hermes half an hour earlier. "Now close your eyes and I want you to put your mind into the centre of your body, into the space behind your navel."

She felt her mind sink and she followed it with her breath. This was an exercise she had learned from Hera, somewhere, sometime, she was not really sure. It was as though she had breathed through her abdomen all her life. It was so natural to her.

The Hierophant shifted his body to bring his index finger to point at the centre of Eve's forehead - the third eye. For the next minute he watched as Eve relaxed into her breathing then he closed his eyes and spoke.

"Do you feel the warmth?" he asked. They both had their eyes closed.

"Yes, my mind feels like it is expanding. I'm sucking the energy from the universe into my navel and… I can see all around me, oh, it's beautiful. I can see the courtyard, it's all sparkling… and strange." She stopped talking and her smile grew larger. "I can see little creatures, they live here too and I never noticed."

"These are elementals that help the guildsmen and women keep the Kingdom healthy," explained The Hierophant softly. "There is one waiting for you to notice her…" He removed his finger from her forehead, resting his hands in his lap, quietly awaiting her reply.

Eve moved her head from side to side as if searching in her mind.

"I think I see a mole… it is a mole, it's a female mole, Molly. She's telling me she knows Hera, the High Priestess… and Mage Hermes. In fact, she knows you, the King and Queen… she knows a whole lot of people in the Empire. She's invited me to accept her as an ally, an elemental ally." Eve kept her eyes closed as she now waited for The Hierophant to respond.

"I would say that this invitation is one you should accept. An elemental ally is rare, there are few with Molly's powers in the Empire. 'Tis an honour to be accepted as an equal by an elemental."

"Oh, she said I can call upon her at any time. I just have to 'see' her. She said I have to go back now, she said my energy is waning and I might get a headache if I don't stop." Eve opened her eyes but she felt disoriented and dizzy. The Hierophant was there to catch her as she leaned sideways out of her chair toppling towards the ground.

The Hierophant spoke quietly of Molly, her new elemental. He explained that because a mole is blind she has to 'feel' her way around. That was why Molly suggested Eve come back to consciousness.

"Molly allowed you to 'see' what she feels as a blind elemental, and that is both demanding and exhausting. This is how you will experience Molly's world, through your senses. Sensory feelings, smells, tastes and sounds. It is three dimensional and somewhat disorienting until you get used to it. Just think of what it would be like to be blind and that's how you should interact with Molly," he said as he reached for the teapot and poured what was now steaming hot tea for the two of them.

"What happened? My head, argh, it hurts right in the middle of my forehead. It felt like I had a horn, like a unicorn's, right there." She placed her index finger right at the centre of her forehead, right where The Hierophant had held his finger.

"I opened your third eye, it was ready to burst anyway. I just helped ease it into wakefulness. But I needed you to centre your breathing at your navel first, that is what allowed you to open your third eye safely," The Hierophant replied.

"May I suggest that you not open your third eye too often, it can make you dizzy and cause painful headaches. Hera is already working on it so it is best that you leave it to her to guide you. If you do it too much when you're conscious, instead of 'seeing' you might just develop a most unpleasant headache."

The two sat quietly sipping their tea as they watched the blackbird return to the birdbath. The bird splashed to its heart's content. By now Eve's headache had disappeared and it was time for her to go to lunch with Mage Hermes.

"This tea is so hot, how did you do that?" exclaimed Eve.

"I used your life force which you had centred at your navel. Maybe Hera will teach you how to do that, too," smiled the Hierophant as he lifted his cup to his lips.

"My dear daughter, today you have made a friend, a special friend. Molly has no power for fighting evil. She does, however, know things, her wisdom exceeds most elementals. Therein lies her power - knowledge is power. Molly knows how to find the answers to secrets and I think the High Priestess may have had something to do with your meeting today. Perhaps you can ask her tonight when you see her," said The Hierophant, looking intently at Eve's relaxed features now her head was clear.

"But it's so hard to see her," she replied softly.

The Hierophant smiled. "Ah, perhaps a little time with Molly may rectify that."

With an impossible leap Eve's visitor was standing beside the birdbath. He flashed her a smile and the blackbird took wing. The Hierophant was gone.

Follin's meditation – Seven of Pentacles

In his meditation Follin saw the image of a man working in the fields. It looked like he was bored or tired, or perhaps despondent.

'He looks like he feels overwhelmed for some reason?' thought Follin.

Sitting in the sunshine in his inner world hermit cottage, Follin closed his eyes and enjoyed the sense of peacefulness and stillness. His old hermitage was always a calm place to visit in his meditations. He brought the seventh image into his mind's eye. When he opened his eyes he was in the field with the young man in the picture.

"Sir, what is it that tires you so?" asked Follin.

"Oh, hi, I didn't notice you watching me," said the young man. He appeared to be a little startled but he was obviously so tired he would not have noticed anyway.

"I've just finished weeding this crop, I've put everything into it but wonder if I did a good enough job," the young man sighed.

"You sound like me, sir, every time I do some task I always worry if I did a good enough job or if I could have improved on it." Follin recognised that his own sense of failure was so enormous that it forced him to evaluate everything he did.

Since his time with the Pentacles he had discovered that he made sure to perform his tasks well. He liked it when Master Pew heaped praise on his apprentices.

"Sir, let me look at your work," said Follin to the young man. As he came closer he recognised that the man was himself as a teenager.

"Why, this is perfect, you've done a grand job of weeding. I like how you've heaped the soil up around the roots and spread the weeds on top so they won't sprout again. Nice work, sir," Follin said. As he did he saw the young man raise his head and smile at him.

"Why, thank you, that's really nice of you to take the time to notice. I've given the plants so much extra care today too. I think I might now do some pruning. I'll get the shears out and start over there." The younger Follin pointed to the grape vines to his right, they were somewhat overgrown.

"That's a good idea. And thank you for showing me a lesson on humility and kindness, sometimes it makes a difference to notice the effort someone has put into their work and to praise them for it."

As Follin departed, he heard his younger self whistling lightly, like a bird, free to enjoy the sunshine of life.

EIGHT OF PENTACLES

Diligence, workmanship, dedicated practice makes for mastery.

"You've earned your day off come tomorrow's day of rest," announced Pew one evening as he pulled his shed door closed against the stiff evening wind. "But the time has come to begin your task of locating and firing the ingredients to make your own blade."

Follin shivered with excitement. "You mean I can create a sword blade of my own, from my very own ore? Like a proper bladesmith?"

Pew smiled and his eyes twinkled with pleasure. "Aye, lad, 'tis time you stopped sweeping floors and wiping benches. You've proved that you aren't afraid of hard work nor the heat of the forge. Thou and Justin will be taking up our camping gear and heading into the mountains with me for a few weeks. Justin will have the donkey ready along with supplies come Monday." He nodded to his young apprentice, Justin, who had forged his own blade as part of his initiation some years previously.

"So make love to yer pretty wives while ye can lads," called Master Pew as the two young men jostled each other, grabbing at their gear ready to head home.

The old man chuckled. "If I had a pretty young wife that's what I'd be doing, but alas, a bladesmith's love life is a little boring, even for a sprightly Pentacles lad like..." he paused and cocked his head to the side. "Come to think of it, I've not tried it with any of the lasses from the other Kingdoms, I wonder if it's not too late for me to try now?" The three smiled. Old Pew was uglier than Vulcan, the God of the smithy, and he knew it.

"Now get off to yer wives, young lads, and have some fun. Justin, you can tell 'yer two youngun's that they can come on the next trip, if their mother says they've been well behaved." With a slap on the doorpost the bladesmith signalled that their week of labour was ended.

"Eve, Eve..." Follin called as he returned to their rooms later that evening. Eve came in from the courtyard immediately sensing that Follin was excited about something.

He kissed her then picked her up and swung her around. Leading her to the courtyard he told her of his trip up into the mountains with Pew and Justin to forge the iron for his own sword.

"Eve, we have the whole day to ourselves tomorrow. We can do whatever you want," Follin concluded.

Follin was left in no doubt that his wife would miss him very much.

At sunrise on the appointed day Master Pew led his small group on their adventure into the Hindamar Mountains. Behind them walked the smithy's donkey loaded with equipment and a fortnight's supply of food.

Captain Bleecher was satisfied with their route. It would take them along secret ways known only to the Pentacles Mountaineer

Commandos and the foresters who collected and sold herbs and other forest materials to the Pentacles craftsmen and women.

When the captain asked if he needed an armed escort, Master Pew responded, "Anymore'n what we 'ave now will just be bothersome, Captain. I've not had a mishap a'fore and I don't plan to 'ave one now."

"Well, you do have young Follin. Sir Dale has spoken highly of his earth magic so I think you'll be safe enough. But be careful, several bands of Wildlanders have managed to cross the Hindamar Mountains and there may be more wandering about up there."

Although there had been raids on some of the Pentacles farms, and several groups of Wildlanders had been seen within the vicinity of the castle itself, regular patrolling had restored order.

Once under the cover of the forest they began the arduous task of climbing the narrow mountain tracks.

Justin had not stopped smiling since they had left the main road. He began to hum and slowly the melodic tune brightened the forest gloom. His tune was taken up by Master Pew and together the two led a round robin song of travelling free under the warmth of the sun. When Follin eventually caught on to the words and rhythm, he tried to meet its complex metre and beat. Between chuckles and roars of laughter from Justin and Master Pew, they had a three-part song rolling along with their footsteps. Each step kept the beat. When they slowed their pace to work around a felled tree, a rock or ledge, the song slowed to meet their footsteps.

After several hours they stopped in a clearing to make a fire to boil their billy, it was time for their morning cup of tea. They sat quietly to enjoy their tea and a snack of honeyed biscuits that Pew's wife had prepared for them the night before. Later, when they settled for lunch, they fried up a 'traveller's meal' of dried meat and grapes ground together with lard, salt and spices. As horrific as it appeared, Follin loved it and had to be reminded that their supplies needed to last a full two weeks.

"The young sir wants to eat everything on the first morn', Master Pew. I think even Donkey knows better'n that." Justin winked at Follin, together they laughed for the joy of living. The feel of sweat on their brow, the bird calls among the forest giants and the smell of fresh mountain air, combined to make their hunger brighter, the sky bluer and the forest greener.

"Master Pew, is this what you had to do when you were an apprentice? You know, go up into the mountains to find your own ore for your first blade?" asked Follin resting with his back against a thick tree trunk after their midday meal.

"Aye, I did. My master was a gentle man but he made me find every scrap of mineral by meself. He not once helped nor pointed out any clues. 'Twas the same for young Justin 'ere, and 'twill be the same for thee. When we get to the plateau, ye'll cut thee a witching stick and dowse the direction ye must go to find your ore. Once ye have a bag of ore ye'll dowse for your kiln site."

"I took three trips into the mountains before I found everything," added Justin after pouring another cup of tea. "I'm a terrible dowser but I did it nonetheless. Master Pew did it in one trip only. He's a Master Dowser, too, you know."

"I didn't know that smiths were dowsers?" mused Follin.

"Aye, there be dowsers in every craft and guild, lad. Some use it to divine water, some to find 'erbs, some to find minerals and others to find the largest deer for their cooking pot," replied Pew.

After several days of hard climbing they finally stopped to rest on the bladesmith's forested plateau. Follin was duly sent into the pine forest to find his witching stick. Pew had deliberately sent him in the opposite direction to the one he knew he must go.

'No sense in making things easy for the lad,' he thought.

Follin found himself completely lost. He could not get his senses to work or focus so he sat down, closed his eyes and leaned his back against a tree trunk. It was a rare mountain beech tree, almost hidden by the thick pines of the forest. As he settled into his meditation he could 'feel' the tree. His chest hummed with its lively, youthful vigour. Instinctively he asked the beech to show him the way to a suitable witching stick tree, one that would serve him well, to find his ore and his kiln.

In answer he saw a single witch hazel tree not ten yards from where he sat. He could feel its proud and youthful zeal. It slowly dawned on him that the beech and witch hazel trees were friends. The two trees shared their time in conversation, swaying in harmony to create an atmosphere of serenity that extended well beyond their leafy canopy.

Smiling to himself he thanked the beech and sought to connect with the witch hazel tree. Immediately an invitation came for him to take the branch he would see when he stood in a certain position.

Follin stood exactly where he was directed in his vision and spied the witch hazel tree's gift, a beautifully formed 'Y' branch. He knew that it would suit his purpose to perfection.

"*Thank you. You and your beech tree friend have given me just what I need to fulfill my task. I promise I shall use your gift wisely.*" Speaking softly, he reached up with his knife and made a single, firm cut. Released, the forked branch felt alive in his hands.

"Why, back so soon? What is it thou hast there, young lad? Is that what I think it be?" called Pew in a somewhat shocked voice as he watched his apprentice return. It had only been a short time since he was sent into the forest and yet here he was with a fine witching stick in his outstretched hand.

"A young beech tree showed me where to find it. The witch hazel tree then showed me the best fork to cut," replied Follin, smiling proudly.

"You've only been gone for ten minutes, not even long enough for the billy to boil." Justin was excited but waited patiently for Pew to hand him the stick to feel for himself. When he felt it in his hands he sighed, "Oh my, Master Pew, this is a beauty isn't it? It has a life of its own."

"Aye, 'tis a bit of a miracle. I sent yon lad off in the wrong direction, yet he comes back with a stick worth ten times what I sensed myself in the other direction." Pew pointed to where he knew was a stand of witch hazel trees not far from their campsite. As he handed the witching stick back to Follin he slapped him on the back warmly. "Nicely found lad, we'll be following thy lead from now on."

That day was particularly hard going and Donkey did not take too kindly to the pace they set. He was tired, becoming more sullen and stubborn with each step. Neither Justin, Pew nor Follin could force him to walk faster. The more they pushed, the more Donkey pressed his ears back in defiance. But Old Pew knew a few tricks, one being that Donkey loved to listen to their songs. So, once again, the three struck up a tune and within a few bars Donkey had his ears up and walking with a spring in his step beside the three men.

"If donkeys could smile, I'd say old Donkey here would be smiling all over his face," said Justin as he tickled their beloved donkey's ears.

Late that afternoon Pew led them up a slippery scree slope to a cave above the plateau. It had been a long, hard slog to the cave mouth.

"We be safe 'ere," wheezed Master Pew. "We'll easily hear a Wildlander, wolf or mountain lion trying to climb those rocks in the dark."

The three sat quietly resting on a rock ledge just outside the cave mouth with Donkey hobbled on a flat patch of sparse grass nearby. Below they could see the kingdom spread before them like a map.

"There be the castle out thataways. And there be the river and lake, ye can see that well enough. And in that direction, somewhere in the haze be the Emperor's home." Pew chewed on a straw that he had kept for himself after feeding Donkey his meal.

"This 'ere be one of the 'old one's' caves. We don't come up here often, in fact, lads, this be only the third time it's had a visit since I was an apprentice. Even the mountain hunters leave it be. They say it's haunted by spirits of the mountain, earth spirits. But we smiths are people of the earth. We create beauty and the earth spirits be our friends."

Pew turned to his two apprentices. "Tonight we'll be doing earth magic. I've not shown thee, Justin, not this magic. It should only be used under certain circumstances and in certain places, this be one of them. In fact, lads, this cave be the perfect place to show thee. 'Tis here I was initiated by my master many years ago."

Just as the sun was setting it turned bitterly cold, so the three men spread out their sleeping blankets beside the fire in the cave. They threw more branches on the flames to keep themselves warm and to invite the earth spirits. Donkey was content to graze around the cave mouth, though sometimes he looked around as if he expected company too.

Before he began the ceremony Master Pew solemnly washed his face and hands then dried them with his rag. He then went to each of his apprentices and proceeded to wash their hands and wipe their faces as well.

"We'll likely meet the King and Queen of Pentacles tonight. The least we can do is show respect by washing ourselves free of grime."

Master Pew hummed to himself as he threw another log onto the fire, then began a slow chant. This led to a smithing song the boys had heard the old master sing while working at his forge. It was a song of pleasure, the joy of being in the flesh and working with the gifts of the earth and fire. The song turned to new words of flesh and bone, rock and soil, ash and smoke. As he sang other new words appeared, words of the minerals found in the earth, of gemstones, ores, sweet limestone, clays and coloured ochres.

The song went on to combine with the warmth of the fire and the flickering of the flames. Slowly the three entered a light trance. As they did so they saw a small humanoid creature, no larger than a small dog, leap to stand before them at the fire. The small male earth spirit joined the old man and his apprentices in song. After a few minutes he turned to invite others of his kind to join them. Eventually, there were a dozen small creatures, clothed in animal skins, dancing and singing in the firelight.

The song shifted in tempo as the earth beings danced faster with swirling, twisting leaps, just like the flickering of the flames. As they danced Follin felt himself being drawn deeper into their earthen cavern. His back eventually touched the far end of the cave and pushed firmly against solid rock. But it did not stop there, he felt himself drawn into the rock itself.

This was similar to some of the experiences Follin remembered from his meditations with the High Priestess. Not that she had ever pushed him into a rock. This sensation of timelessness was very much akin to what he sometimes experienced in her Sanctuary. He relaxed knowing not to fight it. He was wise to these sensations and moods of the spirit, so he let go.

Justin was confused. He knew he had to go with the experience but he immediately became fearful and began to struggle. His master had prepared him beforehand but, even so, the sensation of melding with the earth itself was almost too much for him.

It was then that Justin saw the King of Pentacles sitting on his throne beside the Queen. They looked at Justin, smiled and nodded. It was in that smile that he knew this was another initiation, the initiation to become one with the Pentacles Kingdom, of the solid earth. This was his birthright, he was born to experience the gifts of the earth as a bladesmith. He could now let go.

———

Early the following morning Donkey snuck into the cave and nudged old Pew with his nose, ready for his breakfast. Finally, Pew sat up and looked around. He collected a pot of wild mushrooms to break their fast then woke his two apprentices still wrapped in their blankets next to the fire's glowing embers.

"Look lads, footprints, little ones like a child's. It looks like the earth spirits had a grand ball last night." He pointed to the many tiny footprints in the dirt around them. "I don't know about ye lads but I feel like a young man again. My, my, I'm starved too. Come on, get up, lads, and let's get to what we came here for." Pew's voice was strong, youthful. As he toed Justin he started to sing. This was a '*get out of bed and get into life*' song that he often sang at the start of the day in his smithy. The boys joined in singing lustily as they rolled their blankets and prepared for breakfast.

Over their morning meal the three discussed their experiences of the night before. Each had his own version of his entry into the underworld of the earth spirits and the insights he had gained.

"I saw exactly where my ores are to be found, Master Pew. I can see it in my mind's eye. I spent all night dreaming about how best to fire the ore, to mix the clay and where to find the dry timber to make our charcoal," exclaimed Follin as he flipped the unleavened barley and buckwheat pancakes onto each plate to sit beside the pile of wild mushrooms. "The earth spirits showed me. They took me to each location and said they would guide my witching stick. They said I was sure to forget when I woke up. Maybe they know something about humans then, hey," he said with a grin.

"What did you get up to, young Justin?" asked Pew, leaning across him to pour another cup of tea. "I saw you enter the rock, it looked like it took four or five of those earth spirits to push you through."

"I was afraid. I had to remember to let go and when I did it was easy." He smiled as he remembered. "It's coming back to me now. I saw our King and Queen, they helped me enter the earth. When I was inside the rock I felt so calm and safe. It was a sense of agelessness as though I was a boulder embedded deep in the earth. I could have stayed there forever. Then I went on a journey." His voice quickened. "The earth spirits took me through all kinds of rocks. I went down into the middle of the earth and swam in molten metal. Then I was flung high into the air in a volcanic explosion, that was great!"

"You what?!" exclaimed Follin, feeling his friend's excitement, "you exploded in a vol…?" his voice faded as he tried to say the new word.

"Yes, it's called a vol-can-o, volcano. It's made of melted rocks. They're white hot, and when the earth can't hold it in, it bubbles up like boiling water. It turns red and runs everywhere. I was shown that each metal has specific properties, and then I was shown the types of soil that hold the best minerals we need for our smithing." He went on, "like, on the other side of the Hindamar Mountains in the Wands Kingdom there are a huge coal seams. Coal comes from ancient plants that died and were then squashed. I saw it happen. This area was once a flat plain that grew enormous forests. Then it all went under the water and the plants were covered with silt from the rains. Now it's pushed upwards into mountains of dirt, rocks and coal seams. Amazing isn't it?"

"I thought I had a big adventure but you've had a much bigger one, Justin. But swimming in Vulcan's pool of molten metal and rock…" Follin put his hand warmly on his friend's shoulder. "I am so amazed you did all that. Now I know what it means to be a bladesmith, even the apprentices are special. The earth spirits must love you."

"Aye, me lad, it augers well for an apprentice bladesmith to have an initiation as powerful as that. Justin, ye'll be a Master Bladesmith soon enough and then people will travel the world to buy yer blades. Mark my word, lad, mark my word." Pew shook his head in wonderment and settled back with his plate heaped with food.

They sat chatting softly in the still morning air savouring their meal of wild mushrooms, pancakes and herb tea.

"Master Pew, if you don't mind, what did you experience?" asked Follin balancing his cup of hot tea on his knee, curious to know what the master had learned in his earth spirit encounter. Through a mouthful of food, Pew told his tale.

"Me, well, let's just say I spent a long time with the King and Queen discussing earth magic and how we need to nurture and use it for our Kingdom's safety. Each of us crafters, guildsmen and women in the Pentacles Kingdom have access to this earth magic, just as mages in the other Kingdoms do. Perhaps not all are as powerful as our craft, though. The smiths, potters and gardeners have their hands in the earth and we all work and weave earth magic, every day. When I was done with the King and Queen I was shown new magic castings and weavings, ones I'd never seen nor heard of before. I'd say my own master, and his master before him, never knew of these magics. I got the feeling that they didn't need them, aye, those were more peaceful times. I was told to teach Justin, but only some of them am I allowed to show ye, Follin. Justin, ye will one day go on yer own private quest to this cave and come back with your own weavings and castings. But, for now, ye have both had some wonderful experiences to make your trek all the more memorable."

They cleaned their breakfast gear and stepped out of the cave and onto the track. Their singing was strong and Donkey swung his head in time with their rhythm.

A few days later, Follin had located his iron ore. Just a small patch, but one that was particularly rich and would only need a little work to prepare for its firing in his kiln. Adjacent was a stand of dead trees, of perfect size for their charcoal making and kiln firing. A little farther was a creek and a bank of clean clay for making the kiln.

"My, this is strange," announced Master Pew, "these aren't normally found together. You said, Follin, that the earth spirits would guide you. I believe you've tapped into more than earth magic young man. Mystic Islanders can do that, you know, and yer part islander and Wildlander, I believe. 'Tis whispered that combination of blood is powerful, it holds the magic of all the elements."

He waved his hand towards the ore. "This patch of ore will produce enough to make many ingots to take back to our forge where ye'll make yer blade, lad. You have strong magic of your own, I can see. Aye, this trip has been a magical one from the start."

Master Pew continued, "We've a few days for the wood to burn down. When we've fired the wood we'll start making light clay to build your kiln. But let's have some lunch first."

While enjoying their traveller's meal, Pew explained the tasks ahead of them.

"Firstly, we'll cut down these dead trees and build the charcoal fire together, it's a big job. Then, Follin, ye'll mine the iron ore and light a separate fire to burn off as much of the organic impurities as ye can. Then ye'll hammer the ore stones into a crumbly powder ready to fire in the kiln. While ye do that, Justin and I will dig a hole and shift that dry clay into it. We'll then wet it, and let it soak, every last grain of clay needs to be wet down. And no stones, we don't want any little stones neither. Justin, I need several armfuls of thin, dry grass to mix into the clay as well." Master Pew now relaxed, his explanation complete. "I expect that by tomorrow afternoon we'll be ready to start building the 'dragon'. That be thy kiln, Follin."

"I remember doing this on my last journey, Follin. Your dragon kiln will be marvellous, this is the best time of all." Justin was so excited that he spilt his hot tea on his leg and he jumped up with a start. When he saw the concern on Follin's face he exclaimed, "It's a good sign, Follin. We smiths have a saying, 'hot burns, hot transforms'. Spilling hot tea means that our smithing will be a success."

Follin joined Master Pew and Justin to cut and cart the dry timber to the clearing they had prepared. There they would burn the pile of dry timber to make the charcoal for his kiln. They built an enormous bonfire and lit it right at the base. Once it was burning fiercely they began slowly to cover the entire pile of timber with soil.

"Won't that put the fire out?" asked Follin as he watched the smoke pouring through cracks in the soil which now covered the smoldering fire.

"Aye lad, that it will. But the coals will turn the wood into charcoal. We don't want to burn it now, we need it for the kiln. Charcoal burns longer and brighter than just plain wood. It's exactly what we've been using in our own firepit in the smithy. We buy it from the local charcoal makers back home. If we had to make charcoal every time we fired the kiln we'd have no time for smithing. All smiths use it, we'd never make a living if we had to rely on burning wood alone. Wood doesn't heat the metal to the temperature we need."

Pew pointed to the spiral of smoke rising from the pile of dirt and wood. "By covering the coals we allow the fire and the wood to do their magic. Everything we do on this trip is founded in magic." He stopped and wiped at his brow with the back of his hand. "Before I forget, we'll need a blood ceremony to bless the kiln before we start. Follin, I'll be openin' you up for that," he said winking at Justin.

Follin gasped, "What? Are you going to cut me open, with a knife? Open up my stomach? No, that's not right... is it?" he asked, his face turning pale.

Justin laughed. "Follin, Master Pew will just nick your hand. The blood will drip onto the kiln and your blood seals the pact between the apprentice and his craft. No crafter worth their salt would dream of failing to wed their craft's magic to themselves." Justin smiled knowingly.

Follin went back to his task of roasting the iron ore stones on his own fire. Then he crushed them with a hammer after they had cooled. As he worked steadily through the afternoon with his firing and crushing, Justin and Pew dug a deep, rounded hole and began filling it with dry clay. Then came the slow process of carting water from the creek and adding it to the clay. Justin took the role of stomper, squishing the mess of slippery clay with his feet.

"I say, lad, you're better at it than me. You can stay stompering while I gather the dry grasses... and don't go fallin' over neither." Master Pew was past the age where he would prefer the easy task of mixing clay to cutting and gathering armfuls of dried grass. Besides, his arthritis was playing up after building the charcoal fire.

"Follin!" he yelled from across the stream, "make sure you've burned all that ore, there's enough for ten pounds of wolf ingot there."

The following day the ore was roasted and crushed. The large fire mound was still smoking and the clay was wet and ready to build the kiln.

Pew stood up from washing his breakfast plate and cup in the stream and called the boys over.

"Right, lads, today is the day. Follin, grab yon witching stick and locate yer kiln site. I'll then show thee how to build yer dragon. An apprentice's dragon is wild, it only exists in the open air, not like our forge which sits tamely in the smithy. Justin, ye can now start mixing the clay with the straw." Master Pew straightened and looked around. "We'll first clean up the campsite then we'll each have a wash in the stream and change into the ceremonial clothing I had ye bring."

Turning to Follin he said, "Today, Follin, is the day of your initiation into the craft of bladesmithing. Follow my instructions to the letter and the next few days will be the most memorable of thy life."

Locating his kiln site was easier than expected. As Follin reached for his witching stick lying on the ground beside his sleeping blanket, it spun and pointed to a clearing not twenty yards away. Follin thanked the invisible earth spirits and, picking up his witching stick, he walked in the direction it pointed. Sure enough, it led him to the exact place it had indicated before he had even touched it.

"Right, lad, now we clear it free of twigs and leaves," said Pew drawing a circle on the ground with a stick. "Dig a shallow pit and clean it up. I'll send Justin over in a minute then I'll show thee how to build thy dragon."

Follin walked into the bush and collected a bundle of thin sticks. He expertly twisted them into the shape and form of a simple hand broom. Briskly he swept the area clean of twigs, stones and leaves. Then he dug a small hole with his spade, just as Master Pew had shown him.

By the time Justin arrived with his first batch of clay, Follin had his kiln space ready. Pew squatted gingerly on his haunches and began building the first layer of clay around the sides of the hole, then another on top of it. The clay wall coiled upwards like a snake that would eventually create Follin's kiln, the traditional initiate's fire-breathing dragon.

"See, lads, ye put the clay down and pat it firm. Keep it tight, a kiln that makes the dragon's breath shouldn't be too big nor too small. The next layer goes on top and so on till ye get to waist height. Slow is better than fast. Think of yer kiln as if she were thy wife. She needs a tender hand, not too firm, but not too soft, neither. Keep thy hand wet and slide it across like so." Pew demonstrated as he spoke. His clear demonstration made Follin feel confident that he too could build a kiln just as well as any other bladesmith.

The kiln grew before his eyes as he packed each layer of clay to rise one on top of the other. The straw helped hold its form and by late afternoon it was finished. Pew instructed him to cut openings down at the bottom and, near the top, a hole for the earth spirits to watch. He then brought out a leather bellows with a clay-fired pipe and showed Follin where to cut its hole at the base of the kiln. Together they sealed the edges around the clay pipe and then prepared the large opening section to go back in, as the kiln's door. This was their access point to remove the iron 'wolf' once the firing was complete.

The following morning, Follin was instructed to build a tinder stack inside the kiln ready to be lit. Master Pew walked around carefully inspecting the kiln's integrity and the tinder within.

"Perfect, me lad, that's much like mine and Justin's when we were apprentices. In fact, I'd say yours has a finer touch to it." Pew explained further. "We like to call our mountain kilns 'dragons' because they are untamed. We've no walls nor roof to control our firing environment. We can't control the wind, the air temperature, clouds, rain or even the amount of sunshine. A wild dragon is just as hard to control. We have to continuously watch it otherwise it could destroy our work, or even cause a wildfire forcing us to flee the mountains. A wild dragon is hard to tame, but today, Follin, ye'll learn how to control thy dragon and his fiery breath."

When he had finished his inspection, Master Bladesmith Pew drew a series of images on the ground.

"See these symbols, these are magic symbols of our craft. Ye're not to show them to anyone who is not a bladesmith. Not even to a blacksmith, they don't know bladesmithing magic neither." He then instructed Follin, "Take your knife, it has to be thy own knife and thine own hand what carves these symbols into thy dragon."

Pew called for Justin to join them. The two stepped back allowing Follin to carve the symbols into the kiln's surface. They were exact copies of those in the dust at Pew's feet.

Next, Pew held out his hand and Follin reached up to grasp it. Pew pulled his apprentice to stand before him, but he did not let go of Follin's hand. He held out his other hand, palm up, for Follin's knife. This was the moment Follin had been dreading.

"With thy blood, I join thee to thy dragon. Thus be the melding of blood, earth, fire and metal." With a flash he cut into Follin's hand and held it as the young Mystic Islander's blood splashed onto the kiln surface. The three watched as the blood ran down to puddle at the base of the kiln.

Pew then reached into his pocket and withdrew a small jar of black balm which he spread over the cut, saying, "this'll help heal the cut."

As he released his apprentice's hand he began to sing. Justin joined him with a soft, gentle harmony. It was not a song they had sung before, yet Follin felt he could recognise the tune from the songs the earth spirits had sung at the cave.

"Lad, light the fire, this be the dragon's breath needed to create the wolf iron."

Justin, as ceremony dictated, handed Follin a hot coal wrapped in bark. Leaning down on the ground Follin gently placed the red coal beneath the dry tinder and blew. His breath caught the glowing coal and it came to life, setting the dry tinder alight.

At that moment Follin felt his heart leap inside his chest. He felt so happy that he hugged his master and his friend, Justin.

Once the fire was well alight, Pew handed the witching stick to Follin. He nodded to Follin who then threw his stick into the fire. Together they witnessed its union with the flame of the dragon's breath that it had helped create. With the final step of his initiation complete, both Pew and Justin whistled loudly in delight, slapping Follin on the back in congratulations. Justin was then sent to the campsite to bring back a rag to bandage Follin's hand, and a bottle of mead from Master Pew's pack.

"Lads, may this be the first of many celebrations." They each sprinkled mead onto the kiln in libation to the earth spirits. "When we finally beat the wolf into ingots ready to transport home we'll finish the bottle. So enjoy what's left in yer cup today because we have plenty of work to do before we start feeding this dragon in earnest."

For the rest of the day Follin carefully fed the fire to dry and harden the clay kiln. This was not the fire they wanted for the ore, that would begin at break of day on the morrow.

They woke well before dawn to fire up the dragon. Today was the day Follin would exercise his bladesmith magic - turning raw ore into wolf iron. Once they were back in the smithy they would turn this same wolf iron into Follin's steel blade.

"Load up the kiln in layers, charcoal followed by about one-tenth iron ore. Justin, stay on the bellows 'til Follin relieves you. We've got to get this to temperature and keep it there all day and well into the night."

Master Pew was so excited that, unlike his apprentices, he had not yet finished his breakfast. He was still eating his porridge balancing his cup of tea in the hand that held a hunk of stale bread - all the while directing his apprentices to their tasks with the other.

"We've got to get the dragon up to temperature to bleed the ore of the last traces of impurities which can weaken a blade. This fire-breathing dragon you've created, Follin, is a hungry beast. Ye'll learn what hard work is today, lads."

Putting down his tea cup, Pew finished his breakfast, stood and stretched then walked around the kiln. As he approached he began a slow chant. It was similar to the chant he had used earlier to imbue the kiln with magic, the magic of a Master Bladesmith. Justin and Follin caught the rhythm and joined him. The beat of the bellows made the chant echo through the still morning air. The frost that had settled on their blankets began to steam in the first rays of sunlight just as the warmth of the dragon warmed the boys' hands and their bodies.

As Master Pew ceased his chanting he held aloft a small box.

"Master Pew, what's that?" asked Follin softly.

"That, me lad, is magic, pure Pentacles magic. This be the core of our bladesmithing, the mineral ingredients needed to turn the wolf iron into steel. Weapons need to take an edge and to keep their edge through battle. In fact, through many a battle. This little box contains a powder that has come from t'other side of the mountains, beyond the Wildlands. One day you, Justin, will need to trade for a box of powder just like this. It's a blend of minerals that are our craft's secret. When you're ready, Justin, I'll teach him how to mix it and use it. Perhaps, Follin, if you stay in our Kingdom and pass through yer apprenticeship to the end and become a master bladesmith, ye'll learn its secret too. But today, my gift to thee is to sprinkle this blend and mix it with yer ore. It will produce the most sought-after weapon in the four kingdoms, aye, and beyond."

As he resumed his chant Master Pew gently pinched some of the powder between his fingers and mixed it lovingly into the crushed ore beside the kiln. His chant changed and he moved up an octave and increased the beat. Justin pushed his bellows to pump the air into the kiln to meet his master's rhythm.

The kiln roared like a ravenous, fire-breathing dragon. Throughout the day Follin took care to feed the correct proportions of charcoal and ore into the dragon's hungry mouth.

It was hot, hard work keeping the dragon fed. By late that afternoon Master Pew told the boys to slow their bellows pumping, to 'ease the dragon's breath'. Carefully he opened the door to the kiln. Its lower belly was exposed and they all looked inside to see the liquid slag dripping onto the ash at the base of the kiln.

"Lads, step back a little, give me some room. Justin, get back to the bellows and start yer pumping, keep it slow and steady. Follin, fetch me yon leather gloves and the long tongs... Look, down in there, can ye see it? In the dragon's belly be the wolf, the iron wolf from which ye'll make thy blade."

Pew poked into the white hot ashes to reveal a lump of solid iron and instructed Follin in how to retrieve it. Throwing the wolf onto the steel anvil, Pew began to hammer it while Follin twisted and turned it, just as he had learned in Pew's smithy.

"Right, now lad, you take over. I'll hold and turn while ye beat the wolf into submission. Then we'll continue into the night feeding the dragon and making wolf ingots. By morning ye'll have enough wolf to make thy sword," grunted Master Pew.

Follin's face was red and the sweat poured down his cheeks to drip onto the ground as he steadily beat the wolf.

All that night they fed the dragon, periodically removing lumps of wolf to beat into ingots for transport back to their smithy. At first light the following day, Follin solemnly broke down his kiln piece by piece to uncover the final lump of wolf iron, hidden in the very depths of the dragon's broken belly of slag and ash.

"Lads, that's it. Well done and I must say this has been the most successful firing I've ever had the honour to be part of. This wolf is the best quality I've worked with, too. I can only guess that the sword it produces will be the most precious I've had the honour of preparing." With that, he pulled his shirt off and threw it into the stream. He then called for the boys to strip off and join him in the cold mountain water.

"This be the cleansing, lads. Once the last wolf is drawn and beaten, the dragon's body broken down, 'tis the time to wash the grime from our skin and to leave this place of magic in peace."

By full sunrise they were seated beside their campfire waiting for the billy to boil water for their tea. They had already fried the last of their traveller's meal and eaten it like wolves themselves. Even though they had lived on it for most of their time in the mountains it tasted simply divine after twenty-four hours of around the clock smithing. Their stomachs satisfied, they curled up in their blankets and slept through the morning.

A flock of little birds hopped about their campsite competing for the scraps and crumbs of their meal - but no one was awake to enjoy their carefree antics.

Follin's meditation – Eight of Pentacles

The parchment in Follin's pocket had become tattered and so he had left it at his bedside rather than carry it around in his pocket. He remembered that the picture for this meditation was that of a master craftsman, carefully carving pentacles outside his workshop.

In his meditation he pulled up a wooden stool and sat down to watch. The tapping of the man's mallet on his chisel was sharp, deft and true. He was so focused that he did not appear to notice Follin watching him.

"Master, may I ask you a question or two?" asked Follin softly so as not to startle the man.

The craftsman looked up but his mind remained focused on his task.

"Yes, you can ask me a question, but not now, wait until I'm finished, thank you." The man's command was firm but polite.

Follin recognised the meditative state the man was in and knew better than disturb him further. He had seen both Master Pew and Justin in the same state many a time as they worked in the smithy.

He recalled how Master Pew would carve swirlings on his sword blades which were both art as well as his signature. The old bladesmith could barely read or write yet his inscriptions were a sought after treasure.

As Follin quietly sat he looked around at the man's workshop. It was smallish, well protected from the weather and he had many pieces of timber in various stages of dress and season.

Finally the man finished carving his pentacle. He blew the shavings from his work and stood to stretch his back and shoulders.

Turning to Follin he asked, "and what is it thee wishes to ask?"

"I was wondering what craft you practice, what be your guild and how long you have been a master," replied Follin.

"An interesting question from someone who is dressed as a smith and obviously apprenticed as one, too, by your look." The man eased back onto his work stool and pulled his pipe and tobacco pouch from his breast pocket.

"Here, do thee smoke?" he offered.

Follin politely declined. It fascinated him, though, to watch the smoke pouring from a smoker's mouth and nose.

"I'll answer thee if thou knows thine own station," said the master.

"I'm currently apprenticed to Master Pew, a bladesmith in the Pentacles Kingdom, sir," replied Follin politely.

"'Tis an honourable craft. Bladesmiths are always in need during times of warfare and Master Pew be the finest in the Empire." He puffed several times to get his pipe lit and then leaned back against the wooden wall of his shed. "I'm a carpenter by trade and wood carving be my love. I was just working on a set of pentacles for one of my customers in the Pentacles Kingdom. You may know her, she is the Queen." The wood carver shook his head in a silent chuckle. Follin knew that he was making a joke because everyone in the Pentacles Kingdom knew the Queen.

"I studied wood carving and carpentry for nine solid years in the Pentacles Kingdom. Then I became a Master Woodcrafter. The Pentacles appreciate my skills and I have plenty of work. Perhaps when you've completed your apprenticeship you could visit me. I might be able to teach you a few things about running a business as a master craftsman."

Follin stared for a moment, then realised that he was in both the inner and outer worlds at the same time.

"Sir, this is real isn't it," he stated.

"Certainly it is young man. Follin, I gather that be thy name?"

"Yes, it is, but how did you know?"

"You bladesmiths think you know everything about everything," chuckled the master, "us wood workers know a few tricks too. Look, behind thee, high up in the corner, see the little bird nest?"

Follin turned to look. Right in the top corner of the workshop was a tiny nest, almost invisible.

"I see it, is that your elemental?"

"It be my elemental, indeed. He teaches me, talks to me, he even takes me places I need to visit for my learning. He also helps me see truth and honour in a man." The wood carver looked intently at Follin then spoke once more.

"One of the problems in any craft," said the Master Woodcrafter, "is young people who think that doing something three times and getting it right the third time means that their learning is complete." He looked directly at Follin. "But it isn't, the learning has just begun. Young people today no longer value excellence, especially those not brought up in the Pentacles craft guilds. Mediocrity is good enough for them and they wonder why their work is not respected."

The Master continued: "There once was a woodcraft apprentice named Argyll. His wise old master gave him a choice: 'I can teach you how to excel at your craft,' he told him. 'It will be a long slow path. Or I can teach you the shortcuts. There will be gaps in your skills and knowledge, but you will finish your apprenticeship in half the time and become a journeyman. You will be earning so much sooner.'

"The apprentice Argyll considered long and hard. 'I wish to learn the deep and true ways of the wood,' he told his master, 'no matter how long it takes'. His master smiled and his long years of training began.

"For the first three months his sole task was to sweep up the shavings in his master's workshop. Then Argyll was given tools to sharpen. The other apprentices were quick to hand over their tools to him, but the craftsmen in the workshop would only give him their old, broken or discarded chisels and planes to practise on. Over time they noticed that even the oldest tools gained a new life. Slowly the craftsmen trusted him to sharpen some of their own tools. The more Argyll focused on his few small tasks the quicker and better he was at doing them. The apprentices still sneered at him. 'Not the sharpest tool in the shed', they called him.

"For six months Argyll not only swept up the shavings, but kept a notebook into which he pasted samples of the different timbers used in the workshop. He recorded their grain, colour, softness, strength, scent and whatever else he noticed about a particular shaving curl. He also kept notes on different tools and how their sharpness or angle of adjustment damaged or enhanced the timber. Then, as well as sweeping and sharpening, his master set him to saw and dress blocks of timber for specific items the apprentices were to make. Because of Argyll's diligence, the productivity of the workshop increased and there was less wastage.

"Toward the end of his first year the apprentices were told to prepare a piece for assessment. Argyll's master took him to the new lathe and spent the day showing him various turning techniques. 'You now have four days to make your own piece,' he said. 'Keep it simple, nothing fancy.' He added, 'your fellow apprentices have already wasted too much good timber.'

"The night before the assessment his master came in late and found Argyll burnishing his piece with a handful of shavings. 'Well done,' he said, 'wouldn't want to overdo it,' he added, wrapping Argyll's piece in a silk cloth and carefully stowing it in the burlap bag over his shoulder.

"The next afternoon the apprentices were admitted into the guild hall to view the results of their submitted pieces. Amongst the large and showy offerings a modest vase sat on the tallest plinth in the place of honour. It was Argyll's.

The apprentices were shocked.

'I don't believe it,' said one of them. 'He's used that rotting old bed post I threw on the firewood pile last month.'

'He's done nothing except cut it and shave a bit off!' declared another.

'Lazy sod has just gouged out its insides,' griped another.

But the judges' comments said it all: 'Excellent example of recycling. Well turned. Minimum waste. Subtle finish enhances the grain."

The Master fell silent and looked at Follin, waiting for his comment.

"So, whatever happened to Argyll?" asked Follin his eyes beginning to glaze over with sleepiness.

"Oh, he went on to become a Master Woodcrafter. It is said that the trees in the forest whisper, 'When my time comes I wish to be immortalised by Master Argyll."

Follin was fast becoming fatigued and the image began to fade. The last he heard before he fell asleep was the man's voice saying, "Follin, visit me again sometime. I'll make sure to have a pot of tea and warmed honey cakes ready for thee."

"But I don't know your name, sir," replied Follin stifling a yawn.

"Argyll," was the Master's reply.

NINE OF PENTACLES
Refinement, self-reliance, discipline, slow and steady wins the race.

The trip home was slow. Donkey, loaded down as he was with the wolf ingots, was not as sure-footed as he had been going up the mountain. Justin gently guided their much-loved beast of burden down the steeper paths. Sometimes the apprentices unloaded the heavier ingots to share between them so that Donkey would not trip and injure himself.

The three sang throughout their trek home. Some songs held magic and Pew taught the boys how and when to sing them. Between songs he questioned Follin on every detail of their adventure, making sure his apprentice understood the procedure of mixing the iron ore, charcoal and the magic powder to make the steel for his blade. He explained that only bladesmiths held the knowledge of weapons grade steel; smiths, in general, knew about iron and casting, but not of mixing the magic powder to make the unbreakable steel needed for blades of warfare.

"Know thy metal ores and clay, minerals and charcoals, and how to mix them, lads. The working is just muscle and rhythm, aye, but the ingredients are the foundations of our magic. When a bladesmith finishes a blade he needs to do it in secret. Do thy hammering and layering properly, it doesn't matter who visits to watch you at your craft - but make sure to keep the final act of magical bindings to thyself." Follin knew that Master Pew deliberately failed to mention certain other aspects of master bladesmithing. That was for true adepts, and even Justin was yet to reach that grade.

Pew continued to drum the craft of bladesmithing into the boys' minds as they reached the valley floor and came to the first of the Pentacles farms. Once among the quietly grazing cattle and fields of grain and vegetable crops, the group could see the castle in the distance. Follin marveled at how much he now missed his wife.

There were no more steep hills and ridges to climb, just field upon field of well-tended crops and pastures for their sheep, milk cows and beef cattle. Some of the farmers called a welcome and wandered over to inquire how the new apprentice went with his initiation. Pew replied that it was an enormous success which augured well for the Kingdom. The old bladesmith was much loved by everyone. He mended their tools when the blacksmith was too busy and he was always there to advise the council during times of hardship.

As they walked past a well-tended crop they came to a fork in the road where sat a farmer and his son. On the ground beside them was a wooden box that moved as if alive. Justin and Follin could not hold back their curiosity and walked across to look. Inside, were five lively puppies.

"Hail, Master Pew and 'prentice Justin. I see ye've taken our hero into the mountains for his initiations. I guess he'll soon be wanting to open his own smithy shop." The young farmer stood and smiled warmly, his small son watched curiously from between his legs.

"So this be Follin, the lad what saved our wagons with his magic?" When Pew nodded slightly he continued. "Then, if I may, would ye mind, Master Follin, to bless my son, Claudie?"

Follin looked at the farmer cautiously, and then at his son, then to Pew. "Master Pew, I've not been asked to bless anyone before. I thought only Kings and Queens did blessings. What should I do?"

"Aye, that they do, me lad. But heroes have good luck and magic, and it would be a fine gesture to bless Farmer Earl's boy. 'Tis something a master is asked to do when he's been particularly successful - or lucky." Pew gently nudged his young apprentice forward.

Follin nervously put his hand on the boy's head, silently asking for guidance. He was immediately struck by a flash of insight and he snatched his hand away in surprise. The farmer saw the reaction and his face went pale.

"Tis bad then, young master?" the farmer's soft voice quivered and his body shook with anguish.

"No, no, not at all, sir. I saw your son as a warrior, not a farmer. He held a position as Captain of the Guard and he was very happy. How old is the boy, may I ask?" asked Follin now smiling to reassure the man and his son.

"The lad be eight years this summer," replied the farmer with obvious relief.

"Then, within the next few years, he will want to join the military cadets where he will quickly rise in rank. He has a strategic mind and will make you and his mother very proud." Before he turned to continue on their way, Follin looked back at the farmer. "Sir, there was one thing more that I saw. I know that your good wife has been unwell, it is because she is with child."

On hearing this the farmer put his face in his enormous hands and a heartfelt sob burst from deep within his being. With tears in his eyes he looked up and grasped Follin's hands in his own.

"I know you have both grieved that she might never conceive again, but she has, and it will be another fine son. A wayward son at that," continued Follin. He held the man's hands in his until Farmer Earl let them go.

Follin looked at the boy, who was now smiling broadly. "Young man, your little brother will love you beyond anything you can imagine. You will need to teach him how to be a good boy and then how to be a fine man when he comes of age. I believe that he will serve on your military staff for a short time. But he will return to the farm to help your mother and father. He, too, will make you all very proud."

There came a whimpering and scratching from the box as one of the pups tried to crawl out. Its gaze fixated on Follin.

The farmer, through his tears of joy, reached into the wooden box and held the pup in his rough hands. "Young master, please accept this fine pup as my gift of thanks. I have sense to know this dog will serve ye well. I already knew that he was for you, he hasn't stopped whining all morning. When ye appeared around yon corner he stopped and went quiet, that's when I knew to ask a boon from thee."

Farmer Earl's voice steadied. "The pup's father is our guard dog, and he's never been beaten in a fight neither. He's protected us from wolves, mountain lions, and even Wildlanders are afeared to come near our farm. His mother is a herder, she rounds up the geese, sheep, pigs and cattle. She even rounds us up when we're too slow." He gave a light chuckle as he wiped his eyes with his sleeve. He then pressed the pup into Follin's chest.

"Please, Master Follin, it would make us proud to know we have repaid your kind gift."

Master Pew stepped forward and shook the farmer's hand. He recognised that Earl was both overjoyed and sad at the same time with Follin's news.

"Earl, you've heard it from our Mystic Isle lad here. If Follin says that ye'll be a father again and that young Claudie will be a captain of our soldiers, then it be so." Turning to the boy, Master Pew said, "Claudie, run and tell your mother that your father has something special to tell her. Now don't you spill the beans of what it is though."

The young boy smiled broadly, being acknowledged by both the Mystic Isle hero and the Master Bladesmith was beyond his wildest dreams. He raced away to find his mother.

"Thank you, Farmer Earl, I am honoured by your gift and I can't wait to get him home to show my wife. We are indebted to you," said Follin, now finding his voice and his manners.

The three continued on their journey towards the main road that led to the Pentacle castle. They took it in turns to carry the pup and frequently stopped to let it run while they walked. Donkey just ignored it.

"Lad, do ye know much about this pup what Farmer Earl gave thee?" Master Pew called across Donkey's back to Follin.

"No, just that it's all white with black socks, that's all I know… and it likes to lick." Follin giggled as the pup licked his face.

"This pup be of a very special breed, very rare. That's why Farmer Earl considered it a gift worthy of yours. 'Tis a 'fae dog'. It sees things, it knows things," said the old man. He continued walking, waiting for his young apprentice to answer.

"Fae? That's a faerie pup? He sees magic and things on the other side?" asked Follin. He looked at his pup with different eyes now.

"Aye, 'tis right. Fae dogs can only be bought at very high price, that, or gifted by the owner. Farmer Earl and his son were on their way to yon castle when they saw us. They waited for you because Earl had that sign. If the pups cried as we approached he would have let us walk by.

They didn't and then he knew to ask for his boon from thee. The question he really wanted to ask was about his wife."

"His wife? But he asked about his son," replied Follin.

"Aye, he did too. But you intuited his real question. Earl's wife has been sickly all of her life. Claudie was birthed with much pain and the midwives thought they would lose both mother and child. Claudie is especially important in our Kingdom, as are his father and mother. They have the only breeding pair of fae dogs in the Kingdom, too. The father of yer pup is a legend in our Kingdom. To frighten off a mountain lion is but one of a fae dogs accomplishments. Thy gift to Farmer Earl was very much valued indeed, one he considered beyond the price of this fae pup."

They had no sooner reached the road that led to the castle gates when a troop of mounted cavalry appeared. The Sergeant directed them to escort the three home and in through the thick castle walls.

"How did they know we'd be there?" asked Follin.

"Lad, 'tis the earth spirits. They told the head gardener and he told the Sergeant of the Guard who told Captain Bleecher. Simple really. Remember lads, once attuned to the earth spirits as we are now, expect strange things to happen." Master Pew then held his finger in the air and continued, "but betray that link, the trust of joining earth and fire at the forge, and the spirits will no longer whisper in your dreams nor guide your hammer. You will be as one dead to them."

When Follin arrived home, Eve was with Alice in the courtyard, learning to sew an evening garment for their next court function. He ran to his wife and held her in a crushing embrace. As they stood in each other's arms, the pup began curiously examining the courtyard. Alice, at first, balked in surprise to see a fae pup up close, then she leaned down to pet it gently.

"Follin! Why, this is a fae dog. That's impossible, there's only one breeding pair in the whole Kingdom," exclaimed Alice, delightedly. "But I should go. No doubt I'll hear the story of your journey and how you obtained the fae pup at tomorrow's dinner. Oh, and I do believe Master Windon is presenting on the situation with the Wildlanders and our crop production. He's always worrying about his farms and insists that the soldiers spend more time protecting them. It's always about money with that old codger."

As she stood to go, Eve pushed Follin towards the bath and walked Alice to the door.

"Alice, thank you for caring for me while Follin was away. I'll make sure we're early, cleaned and scrubbed. Will there be dancing afterwards?"

"Yes, the musicians have been asked to attend. They've been practising and I think Windon's farm workers are going to sing for us as well. It should be an entertaining night. Make sure you wash that Mystic Isle husband of yours properly, I can smell him from here." Alice smiled knowingly as she left.

Eve turned to listen as her husband poured water from their kettle into the bathtub. Bending down she lifted the pup and called out to him. "Follin, who's pup is this? Where did it come from?"

When he did not answer she wandered in and saw a very tired Follin collecting clean clothing and a towel to place beside his bath.

"It was given to me for blessing a boy on the way home. The farmer said it would protect us when we are in danger and herd us when we wander down the wrong path," replied Follin as he wearily pulled off his filthy clothes and threw them into the tub at the back door.

Eve snuggled her face into the pup's soft white fur and whispered, "You've come at the right time, little one, but I wonder what your name is?" She examined his white coat and four black feet. "With a coat of white and feet so black I think you should be called 'Sox'."

Together they heated more water on the fire. By the time Eve had made him tea and a large slice of cake, with cream and honey, Follin was already asleep in the bath. At first Sox stayed by Eve's side while also keeping his eye on the bathtub. But it did not take long before he wandered through their rooms and then outside to lay claim to the courtyard. Eve startled when she heard a commotion outside and quickly ran outside to check that the rooster and his hens were safe. Laughing, she saw the fowls chase Sox around the courtyard. After a couple of circuits they all turned and Sox chased the rooster and his hens. Eve was still laughing when they changed direction again. She went back inside, knowing that Sox would not harm his new playmates.

After their lovemaking the two lay together in bed, talking about what they had done over the past weeks. Although Eve was interested in his adventures it was soon evident that making a kiln from clay and turning dirt into iron soon bored her. Follin politely took the hint and asked his wife about her own adventures. In truth, he was too tired to even want to talk so he contentedly let her guide the conversation in whatever direction she wished.

"After you left I had some time on my hands so Alice decided I needed to learn how to be a good Pentacles wife. She took me to the kitchen and the head chef let me help him. Mind, I did get in the way a lot, especially when they were busy. I learned to skin a rabbit, poach a trout, skim the cream from milk and how to pour a beer without it foaming all over the place." She was so obviously excited that Follin only had to smile to encourage her to keep talking. Soon he found himself fascinated by her story of what she had been doing while he was gone.

"Eve, I don't know how to do those things either. I can't pour beer and I can't poach, in fact, I don't even know what 'poach' means." He pulled her close. "Darling, it sounds like you're going to be a Master Chef too, lucky me."

"Oh no, that's a nine year apprenticeship, no way do I want to be a chef. These Pentacles take things way too seriously. Can you imagine slaving in a kitchen, cooking for a hundred court staff, and royalty, for nine years? No way." She snuggled her nose into his neck, breathing his manly scent into her being. They had been a long time apart. "I didn't spend all my time learning to cook, either. Alice took me to the gardeners too, they've a lovely guild. The court's head gardener grows the herbs for their healers as well as for the table. My goodness, Follin, they know so much. I thought I knew a lot about herbs but the Pentacles gardeners and herbalists know just about everything."

"And I suppose that's a nine year apprenticeship too?" suggested Follin sleepily.

"Yes, everything is nine years in the Pentacles Kingdom. They're so patient and so well organised. Their gardens have rows of perfectly placed plants. They know the right times to plant, trim and pick the herbs too. I knew most of that from my grandparents but the Pentacles Master Herbalist taught me even more about the properties of a herb grown on the dark side of the hill compared to the sunny side. Some plants change their potency and characteristics just by how much sunshine they get and when they're planted."

Follin next asked about her work with Mage Hermes and High Priestess Hera, he was particularly interested to hear about that.

"Every afternoon Mage Hermes came and sat in our courtyard to teach me elemental magic. This time it was Pentacles magic like nothing I'd known before. When it got dark outside he would guide me into a meditation and call up High Priestess Hera." Eve shivered in his arms and Follin held her closer.

"What's so scary about that?" he asked.

"The High Priestess, she's so much more powerful in the evenings, especially when its dark. I can barely connect with her during the day, but at night, my goodness, she's alive," whispered Eve.

"But can you see her clearly yet?" he asked.

"Yes, I can now see her. I asked her why you never struggled to see her. She explained that you had to leave home and go on your journey because you were already halfway across the border of consciousness, where she lives." Eve shivered again. "Hera said that you're very sensitive and were already living in the other world, but you didn't know it. She told me that because of your extreme sensitivity you had to leave home otherwise you would have become sick and died young."

The following morning Alice escorted them to breakfast. She explained that the Pentacles Kingdom held a secret and that secret was sensuality.

"It's not a joke, Eve," she continued over her bowl of porridge and honey. "Our kingdom has produced the best lovers the Empire has ever known. Our lovers have entire libraries written about their lovemaking. How do you think the Swords authors get their stories? They don't make them up you know. They may be smart but they lack creativity and imagination and so have to reply on us for their inspiration." The group at their breakfast table all nodded in agreement.

"We've left some books for you and Follin on your bedside table, we hope you don't mind. If you're going to study what it is to be a Pentacle, then you need to learn to love like one," said Lenny, his face was serious, reflecting his earnestness to reveal the Pentacles' secret specialty.

"In the olden days young couples would have a private love tutor," Rhiannon added. "Yes, the King and Queen would appoint a royal tutor whose task it was to train newlyweds in the art of lovemaking. I can't imagine anyone needing training though... but then again, if you came from the Wildlands or any of the other Kingdoms maybe you would," she giggled behind her hand.

"Well," answered Eve with a giggle of her own, "we are Mystic Islanders, we're not from the Empire so maybe we do need a tutor." She looked at Follin whose eyes widened. "But I guess the books will do, and if we need help we know who to ask," she turned and giggled as she pointed to her friend, "Alice!"

The little group broke up, laughing as they headed off to their day's tasks. Follin and Eve had their own work to do as well. It was Follin's day to begin making his own blade from the wolf ingots brought back from the mountains, and Eve had to get back to her studies with Mage Hermes.

"Umm, did you mean that? That we might need a love tutor? That makes me feel a little... frightened," admitted Follin as he held Eve's hand on their way to the bedroom to change into their work clothing.

"You are so silly!" Eve said coyly chewing on her little finger. "They set us up this morning, didn't you see? Besides, I don't think they know any more about lovemaking than us Mystic Islanders. We've got wild energy which they don't, and that means we can turn it to create anything we want. If we want to make love we do it with a passion and wildness even the Wands can't match. But..." she paused, trying so hard not to laugh at the look of surprise on her lover's face, "if you really wanted, I could ask Alice to tutor us, I'm quite sure she would oblige."

That evening they sat with Page Alice and her friends. At their table Follin noticed how the pages and squires were clearly excited at the prospect of the farmers' singing and the dancing afterwards.

"We approach music like we approach everything," Alice answered Follin's questions. "To sing is to be a perfect conduit between spirit and human. Us Pentacles don't half do things, not like those pesky Wands and Cups. They'll start something but leave it before it's properly finished. And the Swords people, goodness, they wouldn't know how to have a good time if they tried," she exclaimed with a chuckle. Her friends laughed in agreement.

"I didn't know there was so much difference between the Kingdoms. Alice, please, do tell us more," urged Follin, keen to learn more about the sorts of experiences he might have when he visited the other Kingdoms.

Page Lenny answered. "Follin, the Pentacles Kingdom is one of perfection, we like to do things perfectly. We may not be as creative as the Wands; we may not be as intellectual as the Swords; and we may not be as emotional as the Cups; but when we put our minds to it, we don't let go until it is done - properly." He emphasised the word 'properly'. Both Eve and Follin could only agree with him.

"We have such long apprenticeships for that same reason," continued Lenny. "We want to make sure that when we employ a master bladesmith, for instance, that is what we get, a master. Can you imagine a sword blade breaking in your hand in the middle of a battle? The Wands once purchased a batch of swords made in the Cups Kingdom by some pretend master swordsmith. The Wands Weapons Master had to send them to us for repairs. Master Pew spent months replacing the blades. The Wands Weapons Master was furious that he'd been tricked into accepting them."

Page Rhiannon continued. "The Wands do a lot of fighting, they live right next to the Wildlands. Their Kingdom abuts the Wildlands like ours, but where they have open forests and plains we have the mighty Hindamar Mountains to protect us. The Wands have a small volcano and around it is a flat plain separated by a river. The river is deep but narrow and so they have to keep patrolling to keep the Wildlanders away. The Emperor himself spends a lot of time with them, advising and planning the security of the Empire. They really need the best weapons money can buy."

Rhiannon took a sip of wine to wet her throat then continued. "That's why Master Pew and Justin are so very important to everyone in the Empire. They make the best weapons for the Wands Kingdom. The Wands have specially trained soldiers they call the Fearless

Commandos. They do marvellous acts of bravery above and beyond anything the other Kingdoms can do - except our Mountaineers who are recognised as the best fighters in the snow and ice of the Hindamar Mountain ranges. If any of our warriors weapons break because of poor workmanship, well..." she let her voice trail off into silence. No one was left to wonder what she was hinting at.

Follin was fascinated, even Eve had not heard any of this. Page Lenny picked up the conversation. "Rhiannon forgot to say that our Mountaineers are considered the equal to the Wands Commandos. So you see, Follin, we may have some of the best trained soldiers in the Empire but we also have the entire Empire to service with quality food, herbs, weapons, tools, pots and pans, cups and bowls, leather goods, paper for the Swords scribes and wall tapestries for the Kingdom courts. We just don't have enough menfolk to help protect the Empire like the Wands do. We run a small, well trained army but the rest of our men are needed to provide goods for everyone. We are dedicated to serving the Empire with essential supplies, the Wands specialise in defending it."

"But what do the Swords and Cups do, surely they help the Empire in some way?" asked Eve.

"Swords are communicators, they do all the negotiations for trade and peace treaties. They help us trade goods across the Kingdoms, and with the other empires across the oceans and into the Wildlands. They also perform valuable treaty negotiations to prevent wars between the many kingdoms and empires in the land. We aren't the only empire here you know, there are probably dozens of them. Our Swords negotiators are valued far and wide. Other empires will trade enormous sums of money and goods for our Swords specialists. They make the best scribes and trade negotiators in the entire world it seems. They can be a boring lot though, all they do is read and write. Oh, and talk, they'll talk your ears off," he finished to everyone's laughter.

"Don't forget," said Rhiannon, "they write the most romantic books and tell the most engrossing tales. Their stories of adventure and love have made their way into every Kingdom's library and every royal court. There's barely a person who can't recite some of their bawdy stories of romance and adventure, or a sweet love poem."

"What about the Cups Kingdom, what are they like and what do they specialise in?" asked Eve. She was fascinated in discovering this information about her newly-adopted Empire.

"They just swoon and make friends," said Alice flippantly. "Theirs is a Kingdom of family and homemakers. We employ them to be nannies and caregivers to our sick and lonely. They make the best healers and they love children. They don't really get along too well with the others, though. Us Pentacles are too boring and set in our ways; the Swords lack empathy and have little idea what the Cups are on about; and the Wands, well, they actually get along together quite well because both are empathic and have strong passions. But the Wands do get quite frustrated with the Cups always wanting to keep everyone happy and together. The Wands would rather go on an adventure than stay at home and be family."

Page Rhiannon continued. "Eve, you've got to remember that each Kingdom has their own ways and mannerisms. We all share some qualities like love and romance, and we do trade with each other and we get along well enough, but the Cups, well, seriously, we just don't understand them."

With a shrug of his shoulders, Page Lenny tried to explain further. "I guess that mixing earth and water just makes mud. We don't enjoy their homely instincts and their obsession with relationships. We share the fun of love and romance like Rhiannon said, but, well, us purebred Pentacles think Cups are just too dependent on each other. They're a bunch of moody dreamers."

"I guess we'll just have to go to the Cups Kingdom and find out for ourselves then," said Eve. "Follin and I have a mix of Mystic Isle and Wildlander blood in us, we'll probably understand them well enough because we aren't purebred anything."

The Pentacles singers entertained with many of the popular Empire ballads. They also sang songs which originated in each of the other Kingdoms. The dancing afterwards was a very orderly affair. Although there were only brief opportunities for touching, it certainly provided for an exaggerated style of courtship. Alice warned her friends that Pentacles dancing had one purpose and one purpose only - a teasing sensuality that would lead to intense lovemaking - and lots of it.

"Oh my," said Eve, "we don't really need that do we, Follin?" she said, turning to her blushing lover.

There was no tuition in magic that night. Follin and Eve were too busy learning the secrets of Pentacles love, a sensuality that was beyond anything they had experienced before.

Follin's meditation – Nine of Pentacles

Follin put his mind into the ninth picture. It showed a richly dressed lady with a hooded hunting bird, surrounded by flourishing flowers and bushes while at her feet crawled a snail.

'This lady looks like she is on top of the world. Her gardens exhibit a vitality that glows with life,' thought Follin as he began to scry the picture. Within a moment it came to life and he found himself standing beside the woman in the garden.

"Hello, Follin, I see you've come to visit me in my splendid garden." It was the Queen of Pentacles. She pulled the hood from her falcon's eyes, lifted him above her head and let the bird fly free.

"Hello, Your Majesty," said Follin, aware that they could be either talking within the inner world, or the outer, or perhaps it was a combination of both.

"To answer your question, we are in my inner world. I felt your presence and decided to welcome you here. I wish to show you the results of the Pentacles' dedication to discipline and hard work. Please be mindful that it isn't just hard work that gets results. It involves goal setting and strategic planning, being in the right place at the right time, and even of good luck." She watched Follin's reactions as she let this sink in for a moment.

"Your Majesty, I understand hard work, I've seen the results myself. But good luck?" Follin replied as he looked around at the beauty of the Queen's gardens.

"Good luck is the result of the work that you are doing right now, meditating, setting achievable goals, and working to resolve your internal conflicts. One creates one's fortunes, Follin. Once you have set yourself up for success you must also be ready to take advantage of the opportunities as they are offered. Too many people learn this late in life

and look back with regret on what they believe has been a wasted life." She paused, but Follin remained silent as he processed her words.

"Remember Argyll?" she continued. "What he didn't tell you about were the choices he made from the age of seven when he chose to make wood his profession. Each time his mother asked if he wanted to play with his friends or walk in the forest to collect timber for his father's workshop, Argyll would consider if he wanted the short term pleasure of playing with his friends or work towards his long term goal of becoming a Master Woodcrafter. Argyll had learnt at an early age that the pain of discipline was much less than the pain of disappointment. It was not by chance that his Master sought him out to be his apprentice."

"That's what I did in my time as a hermit. I worked hard on my goal to heal my inner child," replied Follin.

"Yes, and thank you for reminding me. When you have children, I suggest that you teach them these simple Pentacles lessons."

They watched the falcon flying with joyful strokes of its wings in the vast expanse of the blue skies above. Feeling a strange sensation Follin looked down and saw the snail was now on the back of his hand. He held it up to show The Empress.

"This snail, what does it mean?" Follin asked enjoying the sensation of it crawling on his skin. "It reminds me to slow down, that good comes to those who are patient. I wonder, is that its meaning?"

"Yes, the snail represents patience," the Queen said. "She also reminds us of the power of timelessness, being of empty mind..."

"An empty mind?" Follin interrupted.

"Yes, being of no-mind is..."

"I remember, that's the Tao, the path of non-action, not-doing. I carved a picture of the Strength Lady and her lion above my hermitage door so that I can see it every time I enter. It reminds me to be..." he thought for a moment then said with a light chuckle, "to be like the snail."

"Follin, I wish to show you the lesson of the snail in a more practical manner," the Queen smiled as she added, "It is a pentacles thing." She Queen told him to lie on the ground reminding him that there was nothing to disturb him in her garden except his own thoughts.

Follin lay on his back and soon began to sink into the ground beneath him. As he lay there he became aware that he was in a different time, perhaps millions of years ago. He continued to drift downwards in what he realised was the ocean. Finally he found himself lying on the bottom of a shallow sea. Time sped by as silt and dead plants piled on top of him. Aeons passed between each breath. Layers of sediment began to build on top of him and he felt his body slowly harden into rock.

'This must be how the layers of earth are formed...' he said to himself.

"I gave Justin this same experience," whispered the Queen. "It demonstrates how coal was formed over time, many aeons ago. It was part of his meditation in the cave with you and Master Pew, he told you about it I believe."

When Follin awoke he was in his bed. Excitedly he reached for his notebook, 'snails, timelessness, and pragmatic Pentacles.'

TEN OF PENTACLES

Affluence, permanence, convention, tradition, the cycle reaches completion.

Over the next few days Follin worked at crafting his sword blade. Master Pew supervised as he explained the finer points. This was Follin's last task on his sojourn with his Pentacles friends; within a few days he would be travelling to the Swords Kingdom. There Follin and Eve would begin another adventure to learn more of what was set in motion when they had first set eyes upon each other.

"That's it, lad, fold and beat... steady on the bellows... Justin, you can rest up a bit now, we'll be needing your muscles as soon as Follin tells us he's ready," called Master Pew. He held the long-handled tongs turning the ingot right and left as Follin hammered it into a rough shape which looked nothing like a sword.

"Right now, lad, cease thy beating and Justin will heat it again." Pew knew that Follin had the enthusiasm to achieve just about anything he put his mind to, but crafting a blade, that required a master's skill, experience, and, of course, his elementals.

"See that crease there, lad, that's your next fold job. We fold over and over to mix the wolf. The folding creates a... homolong... horromolong... Justin! What's that word I'm looking fer?" he called to his apprentice only a few feet away resting at the bellows.

"It's 'homologous', Master Pew," Justin laughed in answer then resumed his soft humming. It was one of the many tunes he and Follin had learned from Master Pew on their way down the mountain.

"Yes, that word, we have to mix the iron so that it is all... homonglosis... homolongious..." Justin laughed and called the word out for him again. "Damn and blast! I just can't get me tongue around that slippery word."

He pulled the ingot out of the forge and held it once again for Follin to beat. Turning it from a lump of mixed strata iron into one homologous lump was like mixing flour into bread dough.

"By doing what yer doing, lad, the sword becomes a single entity. No amount of fighting will break it. The secret powder I mixed in with thy ore adds strength and durability, it will destroy other weapons but never break itself," continued Pew as he turned the wolf back and forth as Follin beat it with his hammer. The young man's arm rising and falling with the same beat of their smithy songs.

"Master Pew?" asked Follin between hammer beats, "if the Pentacles make swords what do the Swords Kingdom make? I'd have thought Swords people would make swords, too."

Master Pew turned to Justin and smiled. This was a common question and one he had been called upon to answer many a time.

"Follin, me lad, Pentacles are creatures of habit, we are happiest when we're able to do what we've always done, routines and habits we are. We like to work with our hands and to plan things out step by step with no room for error. Look at my smithy, aye, 'tis got a peg for every tool and every tool has a peg. At the end of each day what do we do? We clean up, put everything where it belongs and close up shop. That's Pentacles, we just do things the way they should be done, properly."

Justin, the sweat pouring down his chest as he pumped rhythmically on the bellows, called above the din of the forge. "As my old dad used to say, *'If a job's worth doin', it's worth doin' well.'* If I've heard that once I've heard it a thousand times in the Kingdom. Us Pentacles like order and structure, we even like to stand in line to buy our goods or be served by our clerks. If we get told to do something new we have to research and rehearse how to do it properly first. We'll have none of this Wands approach of *'throw away the manual then try to get it to work'*, only then to go back and try to find where the manual had fallen. Pentacles create manuals for a purpose, and we've been known to take manuals to bed with us."

"But do the Swords people make swords?"

"They wouldn't know which end was the stabbing end, lad. Their soldiers are likely to poke themselves in the eye with a sword. Funny ain't it," laughed Pew. "Swords are Air folk, they think and talk and plan and make up new designs. Swords people specialise in warfare of the mind and tongue. To get to your question, and I know you didn't want all this fluff - they are master archers. Their practical specialisation is flight, using the wind and calculating how to fire an arrow into the air to make it stick into some poor Wildlander. But getting back to the differences between our two Kingdoms, Swords hate sameness and routines. They're the complete opposite to us in so many ways..."

Justin added, "...except they do write manuals, but not as practical as ours. They write manuals about writing manuals. They talk about it while we go ahead and do it."

Follin waited once more for the wolf to heat up in the forge as Justin increased the beat of his bellows. His breathing was deep and his shoulders broad. The three perspired freely in the heat of the smithy.

"We need Swords like they need us," Master Pew continued as he swung the wolf back to the anvil for Follin to continue his work. "We employ them to do our negotiations when we make trade with foreign merchants. No one has ever out-negotiated a Swords trader in my lifetime. They can read a trade or treaty like a book. We use their ingenious inventions, and make them work better, I might add. They make good authors but we can sing their socks off. And, no one makes music like we can…"

"…or make love!" called Justin with a wink to Follin.

"When I go to the Swords Kingdom, what will they get me to do? Do they have bladesmiths?" Follin asked.

"Lad, they'll make thee learn thy tables, grammar and spellin'. They educate, but ye'll be all right with that. We've taught yer the 'how', they'll teach yer the 'why'. They spend an awful lot of time studying, arguing and intellectualising. I'm sure they invented the library so they had somewheres to sit while they debated the very meaning of the word. I'll hazard a guess, though. If 'tis the Emperor's wish you study each Kingdom's magic then they'll teach you the magic of observing, listening, seeking clarity and strategic thinking."

Master Pew decided that the wolf was ready to put aside while they had a short break. "Lads, take a break. Justin, put the kettle on and brew us some of that new tea thy lovely wife sent us."

The next day was to be Follin's last but one with Master Pew, and his friend, Justin. He was not quite sure how to say goodbye but as he scratched Sox under the chin an idea came to him. He now knew what to do to repay their kindness and generosity.

When Follin arrived at the smithy he looked his master respectfully in the eye.

"Master Pew, I am indebted to you for initiating me into the craft of bladesmithing. I know I'll never be a master bladesmith, but you have taught me the value of discipline, hard physical work, attention to detail and the responsible use of earth magic. These are very valuable lessons for me." Follin collected the last of his ingots and stacked them on Master Pew's bench. "I don't have anything of value but these. I would like to give them to you as a thank you. I made them myself and they hold part of my spirit. Please, Master Pew, accept them as a gift from my heart. A small token of my appreciation for your tutelage, your kindness and friendship."

Master Pew nodded slowly then reached for his handkerchief to wipe at his moist eyes.

"Son, the gifting of thy own wolf is beyond my asking. The spirit in which they be gifted are what a master appreciates more than the gift. 'Tis a fitting gift, lad, from thy heart, aye, and it is fitting that I now pass my talented apprentice to the masters of the Swords Kingdom. What thou will do there I am not sure. But I do know that thou will excel beyond thine and their expectations." He blew into his kerchief and wiped at his eyes once more. As he did so he wandered off to the back of the smithy so the boys would not see his eyes watering again.

Follin turned to Justin. "You have been a true friend to me," he said. "You have never bullied me, nor laughed at my clumsiness. You have generously shared your knowledge with me and helped forge my sword. I value your friendship beyond measure. In return I give you this, just for you." Follin leaned forward and whispered in Justin's ear.

As he spoke Justin's expression changed from bewilderment to joy. A huge smile lit his face as Follin stepped back.

"Really?" Justin stammered. "That's really going to happen?"

Follin nodded and smiled.

"Justin," Master Pew called, "assemble the materials for the guard, grip and pommel, while Follin and I continue working the wolf."

Master Pew and Follin resumed beating and folding the wolf. Follin's sword was starting to take shape. With a few more beats of the hammer, Master Pew told Follin to step aside.

It was Master Pew's wish to complete the final magic passes that only a Master Bladesmith could perform. He explained to Follin that even Justin could not make a magical sword such as this one until he had completed his apprenticeship. Even then, Pew continued, there were certain things that Justin still needed. Such things that he, a Master Bladesmith, had been gifted, hidden in his smithy. As he spoke he glanced up at the roof, just above the forge. Follin noticed but did not think anything of it.

"Now run along and leave me be, this sword is calling for me to release its power - I ain't doing it with anyone around, the smithy spirits told me so. Go to Master Lexis tomorrow midmorning. He'll have finished yer scabbard, then come back here." Master Pew waved the two apprentices out of his smithy and closed the door.

Justin smiled and looked up at the sun in the sky. "Looks like we've got the afternoon off. Let's drop into the pub and have a pint and some lunch."

After settling themselves at a booth in the pub's dark recesses Justin excitedly asked Follin how he had seen his future.

"I don't know," Follin replied. "It's just something I can do sometimes. When I tried to tell my teacher at school about it I got into trouble for telling lies so I never told anyone after that. When Master Pew asked me to bless Farmer Earl's son I was afraid that I would be accused of showing off or making it up."

They lapsed into companionable silence as they sipped their ale.

"Justin," Follin said quietly. "What did Master Pew mean by saying a Master Bladesmith had special magic in his smithy?"

"He means his elementals. Did you know that I've been Master Pew's apprentice for seven years yet I've not once seen his blade spirits a work? He told me he has two elementals, earthly blade spirits. When his master retired he invited his elementals to transfer to Master Pew. I was hoping that one day, when Master Pew retires, his elementals will choose to work with me. But if he gifts me one of his elementals that would fit in with what you saw me doing in the Wands Kingdom when I graduate as a Master Bladesmith." Justin took another sip of his ale. "Their blessing on the blade is of such power that not a single blade has broken in battle since Master Pew's master's master enticed them to his smithy. Now how's that for power?"

"That is powerful. No wonder Master Pew's swords are the most sought after in the Empire." Follin lightened up considerably when he heard that.

"Why does Master Lexis makes your scabbards. Is that to do with earth magic too?" Follin asked.

Justin stopped pulling ashes from his long, brown hair to answer. "Yes, in a way it is. Master Lexis is the master scabbard and leather worker of our kingdom. If you have a spear blade, you take it to Master Lexis, and he'll bind it for you. He makes weapon belts, knife sheaths and sometimes leather and steel shields, but not often. His magic is 'protection'. His scabbards help protect the wearer, not just the weapon."

"Huh? How can that be?" asked Follin as he handed his empty mug to the serving girl who had just placed their chili bean stew and sour dough bread on the table.

Justin chuckled, "Ha ha, you don't believe me, do you, but it's true. Ask Sir Dale and his squires. They each have one of Master Lexis' scabbards, not once have they been injured in battle despite being beaten off their horses on many occasions. They've always escaped serious injury. Sir Dale has one of Master Pew's swords too, it was handed down from his father. There's not a nick or a scratch to its blade. It's as sharp today as the day it was made."

"Wow, that's powerful magic. I doubt even Mage Hermes could do that," said Follin.

"Yes, that's the bladesmith's magic. But then, Master Pew can't fly through time nor travel the Kingdoms in the blink of an eye, neither," laughed Justin.

"Did you ever notice how Master Pew hummed his songs and moved while he completed the final stages in crafting his swords?" asked Justin.

Follin shook his head.

"Well," continued Justin, "that's how he communicates with his blade elementals, his blade spirits. They live inside our smithy, in a small nest in the timber roof. Master Pew said that they like the smell of smoke from the forge more than anything. Old Master Pew sometimes plays jokes on them and moves their little house when they're busy working the steel. I've seen him. He don't tell me but I know."

The following morning Follin and Justin found Master Lexis sitting outside his workshop enjoying the morning sun. At their approach he stood and stretched. Follin noticed how tall he was, his long brown leather apron and matching leather cuffs, all adorned with silvery writing and symbols. Master Lexis' long hair was silver, too, and it hung shimmering to his shoulders. His green eyes creased with warmth as he smiled a welcome.

After Justin had introduced Follin, Master Lexis led them to the forest behind his workshop. He told Follin to go into the forest alone and find his scabbard.

"I placed it there overnight to reabsorb the tree's energy," he explained. He pointed to a forest track, while he and Justin sat on a large log in the sun.

Follin entered the forest where it was noticeably cooler. He looked around but could not see a scabbard. In fact, it was hard to see anything in the dim light until his eyes adjusted.

After a few moments Follin saw a faint silver gleam in the fork of a tree trunk partly obscured by leaves and branches. His heart sank when he saw the tree's smooth, slippery bark.

'I wonder, would I be able to climb up there and get it?' he thought with a sinking sensation in his stomach. *'It's a difficult climb and I'm not sure even I could do it.'*

He leaned his back against the tree's trunk and slid his body down to sit quietly at its base. Embracing the stillness of the forest and the sounds of muted bird calls around him, he entered a light trance. Follin's breathing slowed as he emptied his mind. Going deeper into quiet stillness he became aware of the tree's breathing.

After a short while the tree said, *'You could break off the branch just above your head and use it to knock thy prize into your hand.'*

Follin could see how this would dislodge the scabbard. At that point Follin wanted nothing more than for the scabbard to be in his hand, yet he hesitated.

"No, causing you pain just for my benefit wouldn't be right."

Follin sensed the tree nod in approval at his reply. The tree leaned toward him. As it came within reach the canopy parted and a shaft of sunlight lit the scabbard and the beauty of its silver inlaid timber was clearly visible. Follin stood and stretched out his hand, trembling. As his hand closed around it he felt leaves gently caress his face. Slowly the tree straightened and the canopy closed above him. He was alone once more in the silent forest.

Follin slowly walked out of the forest, carefully examining his scabbard. Inlaid into the polished timber was a silver caduceus, the proud symbol of the Mage Guild.

"Follin," called Justin the moment he saw the scabbard in his friends hands, "it is beautiful."

Still a little dazed, Follin was silent.

Master Lexis stood with a broad leather belt in his hands. He helped Follin put it on, adjusting the scabbard and securing it firmly at his waist.

"Well done, Follin," he said.

"I don't understand," stammered Follin. "When I cut my witching stick, I didn't think that I would hurt the tree... but today was different."

Master Lexis replied, "The trees know when the creatures of the forest need homes. They provide fallen branches for them willingly and firewood for the warmth and survival of humans. When you took the witching stick it was freely offered. The witch hazel was happy to suffer a little pain to assist your learning. There is an awesome order in the world of nature, but when a tree is cut down without consideration of the life cycles of the forest, it causes pain. That pain ripples outwards into the world."

"So the tree offered me its branch and I could have broken it off..." Master Lexis held up his hand.

"Follin, the tree was prepared to sacrifice its branch for your benefit. However, your deep respect for the forest enabled a more fitting alternative."

As Follin began to stammer his thanks Master Lexis cut him off, holding up his hand. Follin looked into his twinkling green eyes and knew that the scabbard had been created with the love and respect for the forest that lay deep in the heart of Master Lexis's being.

Justin and Follin made their way to the smithy where they met Master Pew striding towards them.

"Well met, lads," Pew said. "Come, Follin, there is one final task for you to complete." He turned and led them back along the road out of town and away from the castle.

Master Pew stopped at the base of a rocky outcrop of granite boulders stretching up its slope.

"Follin," he said, "it is time for you to honour the earth spirits and to receive their blessing upon your sword." He pointed to the top of the boulders and moved into the shade of the trees just off the road. Follin glanced at Justin, who shrugged, and joined Master Pew.

Clambering up and between the boulders was heavy work in the hot sun but eventually Follin made it to the top. He could not see his sword. Groaning inwardly, he found a boulder that offered some shade and sat down with his back to it. As he had done so many times, Follin closed his eyes and went deep into his centre. His racing mind slowed as he heard distant bird calls. He felt the stillness of the surrounding farmland and the timeless solidity of the rock at his back.

Hearing voices, Follin opened his eyes. In front of him were several small earth spirits dancing in the sun. Follin recognised them from the night in the cave in the mountains with Justin and Master Pew. They danced and leapt, looking over their shoulders at him. Eventually, Follin realised that they were indicating that he should follow them. Half way around the hill they paused on a narrow ledge in deep shadow. Follin peered into the gloom as, one by one, the earth spirits disappeared into the rock face.

Follin centred his energy at his navel and followed them, easing his being into the solid rock. It was dark and cool inside. He felt himself settle into the familiar sensation of well-being that always accompanied his earth meditations. The energy within the rock was so extreme that he felt as though he had been struck with a stupefying enchantment.

Time seemed to stand still... with a sudden shock Follin remembered his purpose. Just as he was tempted to fall into the benumbing stupor once more, his arm was grasped by the earth spirits. They guided his hand until it touched an object that sent a chill up and down his spine - he had found his sword.

The touch was hot, almost unbearably so. It burned as his hand closed over the grip and a sudden intoxicating euphoria penetrated his being. He unconsciously stepped backwards to find himself standing on the narrow ledge once more, but he was stuck. The hand grasping the sword was still in the rock. With a rising panic Follin remembered to centre himself. It was only then that he was able to draw his sword free.

Follin turned his back to the rock face, his sword grasped firmly in his hand. With a life of its own, yet an extension of himself, his sword thrust, parried and feinted. In his mind he could see his enemy cleaved in two.

But there is no blood...' Follin thought, momentarily bewildered.

Before him appeared the male earth spirit who led the dance in the cave that night. He spoke into Follin's mind, *'Your blade is not a weapon of destruction but of enlightenment. Go now, and know that we spirits of the earth have given your blade our blessing.'*

As Follin came into view, Justin gasped. With his blonde hair flowing behind him, determined step and his sword in its scabbard by his side, Follin looked like a warrior of legend. Gone were his habitual half grin and frown. His face was serious as though carved from rock.

Justin jumped up and ran excitedly to him but stopped before he reached the stern faced warrior. Follin saw his friend's hesitation and smiled, a glorious full smile. Justin ran forward again and clapped him on the back.

"Justin," called Master Pew holding out his arm. "Come, lad, I need your arm to stand. Walking up and down these hills all morning has wore me out. And I badly need a hot cup of tea."

———

That evening was their last in the Pentacles Kingdom. While waiting for Alice to collect them for dinner the two lovers sat quietly outside in their courtyard watching Sox play a chasing game with Molly, Eve's earth elemental.

"Eve, I can't even see Molly, how can Sox see her?" asked Follin wondering how his fae pup could not only see an elemental but that the two would play with each other.

"It's funny," laughed Eve. Her laughter always made Follin's heart leap. "These two haven't stopped playing since Sox arrived. As soon as he wandered into the courtyard he saw Molly and, well, Molly sensed him. They sniffed at each other and then they began to play and they've not stopped since."

"This is so strange. I've got a dog that plays with an invisible friend, you've got an invisible friend who plays with a fae dog. I wonder what the Swords people will think about it when we get there?" mused Follin as he watched his dog chasing... nothing.

Just on dusk Rooster crowed for his hens to gather at the end of the courtyard ready to leave for their evening nesting. At his signal, Sox quickly scurried around the courtyard to hurry the hens. With a raucous cock-a-doodle-doo the rooster thanked the fae pup for his help. Puffing out his chest in contented satisfaction the rooster escorted his hens over the wall and off to their beds.

Follin and Eve looked at each other in astonishment before bursting into laughter.

"That is no ordinary pup! Not even a fae dog should be able to do that!" exclaimed Follin as he called Sox to come inside with them.

———

Follin and Eve's last dinner at the Pentacles Castle was a memorable one. In planning any activity, including celebrations and farewells, the Pentacles courtiers were thorough and considerate. When Alice came to take them to dinner she explained the order and protocol for each of the events in the evening ahead.

Follin's usual fears of inadequacy surfaced. "I don't know if I can get through this dinner tonight," he whispered to Eve as they followed Alice down the long stairway to the banqueting hall.

"Me, too," confided the normally enthusiastic Eve. "Let's make a mess of it together, shall we?" Follin relaxed a little.

"The Pentacles may have high standards but they are too polite to laugh or chastise us if we get it wrong," Eve giggled.

"They'll probably put it down to our naïve Mystic Island charm," suggested Follin with a smile. "That's what I heard one of the Queen's ladies say last week."

Eve laughed softly.

"Let's smile and laugh and enjoy ourselves," she said. "No one will know that we don't have a clue about what's going on, despite Alice's very thorough briefing." Follin grunted in agreement.

Eve paused, thinking about how best to allay Follin's fears. "I believe you'll handle it just fine and I'll be very proud of my handsome, charming, modest husband."

When she saw Follin frown she added, "You really don't know how gorgeous you are, do you?" she finished.

Alice overheard this last comment and smiled in agreement.

The Herald announced their entrance in grand style and the minstrels struck up an old, rousing Mystic Island favourite they had learnt for the occasion. As they entered, everyone turned and applauded. Follin resisted the urge to look over his shoulder to see which august personage was following. Instead, he followed Eve's lead, nodding and smiling at those on either side of them as they made their way to the table of the King and Queen.

Just as Eve expected there was glorious food, pleasant conversation, wine as mellow as honey, singing, music, dance and speeches. She and Follin were kept busy entertaining a steady stream of well-wishers at their table.

At precisely 11pm, just as Alice had told them, the King and Queen rose, and led them to the private chamber adjourning the hall. As the sounds of merriment were muted by the closing chamber doors, the Queen invited Eve to sit beside her while Follin sat beside the King.

Mage Hermes, snoozing by the fire, awakened at their entrance. With a muffled grunt he drew himself upright in his chair, but his hooded eyes and yawn betrayed his lingering stupor.

Over coffee, and yet more cake, they reviewed Follin and Eve's time in the Pentacles kingdom, both in the outer and the inner worlds of their meditations and dreams.

"Your Majesties and Mage Hermes," announced Eve, "my husband and I are most grateful for all you have done. Thank you."

"My dear Eve, you are like a daughter to us," said the King. "I have one question to ask before you leave our Kingdom." He paused, watching her intently. "Who are we?"

Eve smiled, she had guessed this only a few days earlier. "You are elementals, both of you are Pentacle spirits," she said, looking into their glowing eyes.

It was the Queen who spoke next. "That was well intuited."

Addressing Eve once more, the King smiled and said, "Eve, you are a marvel. Not only are you bright of mind, but your spirit is aligned with the Tarot Empire's. There was no way that you would have been able to intuit that answer without being at one with the divine spirit of our Kingdoms. We've watched you grow from a naive young lass, fresh from the Mystic Isle forests, into a woman of merit."

"Your Majesty, thank you, but I was wondering, are you human as well?" asked Eve, a little breathless from the King's praise.

"You could say that. We were here before humans. When the Tarot Empire arrived the God Pan decided to awaken us into consciousness. We have evolved since that time and now live in both worlds, the world of consciousness and of the unconscious," answered the Queen.

"So you don't sleep?" asked Eve not letting an opportunity like this pass her by.

"You are an inquisitive young lady, but that's why you are here," said the King. "To answer your question I shall ask one in turn: when do you feel our energy the strongest? In your meditations or now?"

Eve did not have to think. "That's easy. When I'm working with Hera and she connects me to your Pentacles energy. It's as though the Pentacles magic consumes me, yet I see you now and you're quite normal. In fact you eat and play and sing like..." Eve paused to think of a suitable description, "...like us. I don't think you ever sleep, but, for all intents and purposes you're as human as I am."

It was the King who answered her again. "Yes, that is a good answer. We simply like eating, dancing and singing. We've spent so much time in our human form that we are... almost human," he said finishing with a broad grin. "In our elemental form we are pure Pentacles earth magic, in our human form we are mostly human."

"But when I am meditating and I see you and work with your magic, aren't you still in your human form?" Eve asked.

"Certainly, we are magical beings, are we not? We may be in our human form but part of us remains elemental. That part is always active and fighting the rot in our Kingdom. Our magic is vigilant, it does not rest nor should it. Without our magic there is no Pentacles Kingdom," replied the Queen.

The King turned to Follin. "Young man, you have a special partner, as have I. My question is: how will you honour Eve's gifts in the task you have before you?"

Follin's face dropped as he struggled to comprehend the question but he was not afraid to admit that he did not know. "Sire, I was a fool at school. I didn't know my numbers or my letters, I couldn't even catch a ball or run without falling over. Tomorrow we leave for the Swords Kingdom and I understand that they know their words and their numbers better than any other Kingdom. I am terrified of returning to be what I spent many years learning to leave behind." Follin looked at Eve and then back to the King and Queen.

"My wife is my life partner. I will love and honour her as long as we are together and beyond, if that's possible. I know things Eve will never know, as she knows things that are beyond my comprehension. So, to answer your question, your Majesty, I am not actually certain how I will honour Eve's gifts in the task set by the Emperor. All I can say is that I know I must support her because the Empire needs us both. If Eve slips I'll catch her, if I slip Eve will catch me, as she has already done many times." Follin stopped talking, fearing he may have said too much.

"My son," said the Queen as she reached across the distance between them, "your answer is more than sufficient. And don't you be bothered by those Swords and their intellect - you now have Pentacles magic. You will be more than prepared to meet the challenges set before you by the Swords. Besides, Eve has Molly, and you have Sox to help you. A fae dog is no ordinary dog."

The Queen looked at Eve for a moment then continued. "Eve, don't expect Molly to take you on her elemental journeys just yet. You are too weak to stay long in her world. Too much time on the other side will exhaust and possibly harm you. May we suggest that you allow Hera and Molly to determine how and when you should work together?"

"I was wondering why Molly disappeared when I worked in meditation with the High Priestess." Eve considered the Queen's words then nodded. "I'll definitely follow your advice, my Queen, and allow Molly to take me on her journeys when she thinks I'm ready. I'll just have to be patient."

The Queen of Pentacles smiled. "Of course, you do know that Molly is one of us?"

Eve frowned and turned to see if Follin knew anything about this; he shrugged his shoulders.

"Your Majesty, I had no idea. I knew she was a Pentacles elemental, but I didn't know she was royalty."

"Ha ha, my dear, no, she isn't of royal blood, but she is a true Pentacles elemental. That means she can communicate with us, my husband and me. If you are in peril all you need do is call to her and she will make every effort to communicate with us. If it is in our power we will help."

The lovers smiled at each other. They knew they had passed the tests set by the Pentacles King and Queen.

As Mage Hermes stirred by the fire, Eve turned to address him. "Mage Hermes, I wish to thank you for your tuition and patience." The mage sat up again politely stifling a yawn with the back of his hand.

"Eve, it is my pleasure to teach you," he said gently. "You must have wondered why I made you relearn much of what you already knew about herbs and healing." Eve nodded. She had, often. "I needed to be sure that you would use the magic as it is meant to be used." He paused. "I have been closely observing you throughout and you are indeed most worthy."

Eve felt relieved, proud and sad all at the same time. "But will I see you again?" she asked in a soft voice. Mage Hermes nodded, his eyes twinkling. He smiled a kindly smile as he sank back into his chair by the fire.

At that the King stood and announced, "Go with our blessing. Know that in your dreams, and in your meditations, we shall meet again. When it comes time to challenge the evil that rots our Empire's foundations, we shall all be united."

At precisely midnight they returned to the Hall. The trumpeters announced their presence. As the minstrels played the traditional Pentacles song of farewell, Follin and Eve followed the King and Queen down the centre aisle between the waving courtiers and their whispered farewells.

At the foot of the stairs the Queen embraced them both said, "You are always welcome in the Pentacles Kingdom. We wish you safe until we meet again."

Follin and Eve ascended the staircase on their own way back to their rooms. Alice stood below looking up at them, a sad, wistful expression on her face.

———

Next morning Follin and Eve said their goodbyes to the assembled castle staff and the many friends they had made during their stay. It was time to go. The sounds of the wagon train preparing to leave called them.

Sir Dale and his patrol were to escort the wagon train loaded with Pentacles goods across the plains to the Swords Kingdom. He asked if Follin and Eve would like to join him up front. Page Alice was with them, with two other pages, carrying their bags and chatting with Eve.

"Certainly, mister handsome Knight of the Pentacles Kingdom, they would like that very much," answered Alice smartly as she smoothed her hands down her tight dress. It covered just enough of her curves to catch many an admiring glance from the soldiers.

"My dear cousin, Alice," said Sir Dale in the bright morning air. "You've spent way too much time partying with those court wastrels. It seems they've taught you some very wicked ways," he said teasingly.

Sir Dale leaned across his horses neck and called to Follin, "Lad, you'll be my squire for the trip. I've ordered Mavor and Allen to prepare for a separate patrol into the mountains. I don't want to spoil your last few days with us."

There was sadness but also excitement at their leaving as Sir Dale called to the wagoneers and soldiers. The cavalrymen were waiting at the front of the train. The horses' breaths steamed in the chill morning air. Nodding to his drummer to set the marching pace, the men-at-arms advanced with a song on their lips, joy in their hearts and a skip in their step.

As they breasted the hill near the castle Follin turned and stood in his stirrups. He bid a silent, fond farewell to the Pentacles kingdom where he had learnt so much.

Follin's meditation – Ten of Pentacles

That first evening on their trip to the Swords Kingdom, Follin sat quietly to reflect on their time in the Pentacles Kingdom. He knew that he and Eve had achieved every task the Emperor and Empress had set before them.

In his final Pentacles meditation Follin studied the picture carefully. It showed a cheerful old man with his family and grandchildren. He seemed happy and content in his twilight years. It said so much of what he wanted in his own life.

Alas, his childhood was one where his father was a kind and caring man but found that he could no longer live with his personal pain, so he had abandoned his family. There were no witnesses to his leaving nor word of him since. Some people said his father had gone from the Mystic Isle to wander the mainland. Some said he went to live with the Wildlanders to start a fresh life. Some even said that he had gone to the secretive isle of Runda.

"Hello, grandfather," called Follin as he stepped into the image itself. "Can you please explain to me the lesson of this image?"

The old man pushed the dogs off his feet and called to his grandson to play with them outside. A small boy, perhaps ten years of age, called for the dogs. Together, with his sister, they ran into the yard, the dogs chasing and barking joyfully.

"The blessings of age are sometimes these that you see around me. Home, food, wealth, family, happiness and fulfillment. For me this is so, but for others it is not always like this. Many elderly live in fear of illness, loneliness, loss of independence and their eventual death."

Follin looked at the man, that certainly was not what he had expected.

"I know, you expected something different didn't you. Something about your father, perhaps? No, this picture shows that sometimes, if one *is careful, if one learns the lessons of the lessons of the Pentacles Kingdom, one might achieve fulfillment in old age."*

The old man stretched and stood up and crooked his index finger for Follin to follow him.

"Young man, see these certificates on my walls? These trophies and medals? The paintings of my children and grandchildren? That's my life history. Those children running around outside are part of the legacy I leave behind. I will leave my house, my family, my craft and my valuable possessions behind when I leave this world. Your father, he left more, he left you. Don't judge your father's actions more harshly than he judged himself. The urge to find yourself is his legacy. Just look at where it has led you: a wife and a world of magic."

As he came back to consciousness Follin remained lost in his thoughts. Happiness was more than just material possessions, he knew that, but what the old man said certainly made sense. However, it did not diminish the pain or sense of loss that the image had invoked within his heart.

The story continues in Book 3
The Fool's Journey through the Tarot
- Swords -

Follin and Eve hope that you will join them on their journey through the Swords Kingdom…

THE PENTACLES CARD MEANINGS - KEYWORDS

The Pentacles are the pragmatists of the tarot deck. They enjoy getting their hands dirty and doing things, making things, fixing things and organising things. Their big challenge is to embrace change while their weakness is their desire to keep things the same. Page Alice is a good example of how Pentacles like order and a set way of doing things. They are traditionalists as opposed to progressives. They excel at ceremony and enjoy having fun but it has to be organised properly first. You can see that when the Queen suggested that they take their meal outside in the gardens. Or when having to move seating to fit Eve in at the table. Their parties are very much arranged affairs and definitely not haphazard. Their opposite element is the adventurous Wands.

Ace - Embarking on an earthly adventure.
2 - Balance, to adapt in the face or hardship, the secret of the 'change point'.
3 - Teamwork, planning, competence, recognition.
4 - Possessiveness, control, selfishness, arrogance breeds stagnation.
5 - Hardship, support, rejection, fearing rejection and loss, failing to notice support when it is offered.
6 - Resources, generosity, power, giving responsibly.
7 - Evaluation, preparation, possibilities, validation, where to next.
8 - Diligence, workmanship, dedicated practice makes for mastery.
9 - Refinement, self-reliance, discipline, slow and steady wins the race.
10 - Affluence, permanence, convention, tradition, the cycle reaches completion.
Page – A smart and excitable youth, versed in the traits of earth magic, willing to pitch in and share knowledge.

Knight – Solid and careful in all his actions, wise to the ways of the world particularly in practical things, brave and reliable, enthusiastic rather than excitable.

Queen – A down to earth and mature woman, practical and feminine, moderated emotions, structure oriented advice – mastery of the feminine Earth qualities.

King – Solid temperament in all situations, quietly spoken and insightful in practical matters, dependable and reliable, prosperity and abundance focused – a master of the masculine Earth qualities

THE ASTROLOGICAL CORRESPONDENCES FOR PENTACLES - THE ELEMENT EARTH

The Four Elements in Astrology

The astrological signs are divided into four groups that represent the basic elements in the western esoteric tradition: Earth, Air, Water and Fire. These correspond nicely with the tarot suits: Pentacles – Earth; Swords – Air; Cups – Water; Wands – Fire.

Earth - Taurus, Virgo and Capricorn – Tarot Pentacles

Earth signs provide the organisation and materials necessary for the other signs to achieve their goals. They are the artisans and workers who enjoy the physical experience of using their body and mind in unison to create for the benefit of everyone.

They are patient and realistic, hardworking, responsible, determined, resourceful, careful, reliable, creative and practical. Earth signs have the ability to turn nothing into something. They are our craftspeople who provide stability and balance so that the other signs have a home to return to, with a meal and a warm bed to sleep off their experiences.

Earth is ordered, structured, down to earth, practical - sometimes they can be pedantic, controlling, materialistic, inflexible and they can become extreme hoarders.

Taurus provides the foundations of the workforce to ensure the job gets done – they can become too fond of pleasures of the flesh like food, alcohol and sex.

Virgo serves to analyse and critique their world – they provide service to others but can become bogged down in time-wasting chores.

Capricorn organises and manages people and processes to get the best from their efforts – sometimes they become overly organised to the point where they control and dominate everyone and everything around them.

The End

ABOUT THE AUTHOR

Noel Eastwood is a retired psychologist with over forty years professional experience in education, counseling and psychology. Now a full-time author, Noel shares his lifelong interests in psychotherapy, Taoist meditation, tai chi, astrology and Tarot. A gifted storyteller, his fiction and nonfiction works blend ancient wisdom and contemporary themes.
You can visit his website and subscribe to his newsletters on the many diverse topics above.
www.plutoscave.com

Other books by Noel Eastwood

www.ingramcontent.com/pod-product-compliance
Lightning Source LLC
Chambersburg PA
CBHW071928290426
44110CB00013B/1517